THE
CELESTINE
VISION

THE
CELESTINE
VISION

*Living the New
Spiritual Awareness*

JAMES REDFIELD

WARNER BOOKS

A Time Warner Company

Warner Books, Inc., 1271 Avenue of the Americas,
New York, NY 10020
Visit our Web site at http://warnerbooks.com

 A Time Warner Company

Printed in the United States of America
First Printing: October 1997
10   9   8   7   6   5   4   3   2   1

ISBN: 0-446-52274-0
LC: 97-61468

Text design by Stanley S. Drate/Folio Graphics Co. Inc.

For all those who hold the vision

ACKNOWLEDGMENTS

Many more people have guided the evolution of *The Celestine Vision* than I can personally thank here. But I must mention John Diamond and Beverly Camhe for their strategic instincts; John Winthrop Austin for his tireless research; Claire Zion for her careful editing; and Salle Merrill Redfield for her ongoing support. Most of all I want to thank the brave souls out there, past and present, who have brought forth the truths that spark our awakening.

CONTENTS

9 LIVING THE NEW INTERPERSONAL ETHIC   141

PREFACE:
OBSERVING THE
TRANSFORMATION

It does not take the mystery of a new millennium to convince us that something is shifting in human consciousness. For those with a perceptive eye, the signs are everywhere. Polls show a growing interest in the mystical and unexplained. Respected futurists see a worldwide search for inner satisfaction and meaning.[1] And the general expressions of culture—books, television documentaries, the content of the daily news—all reflect a growing outcry for a return to quality and integrity and for the rebuilding of a community-based sense of ethics.

Most important, we can sense something changing in the quality of our own experience. Our focus seems to be shifting away from abstract arguments about spiritual theory or dogma and reaching out for something deeper:

the real perception of the spiritual as it occurs in daily life.

When I am asked about the popularity of my first two novels, *The Celestine Prophecy* and *The Tenth Insight,* I always reply that this acceptance is only a reflection of the mass recognition of the specific spiritual experiences these books describe.

Increasingly more of us, it seems, are becoming aware of the meaningful coincidences that occur every day. Some of these events are large and provocative. Others are small, almost imperceptible. But all of them give us evidence that we are not alone, that some mysterious spiritual process is influencing our lives. Once we experience the sense of inspiration and aliveness that these perceptions evoke, it is almost impossible not to pay attention. We begin to watch for these events, to expect them, and to actively seek a higher philosophical understanding of their appearance.

Both of my novels are what I call adventure parables. They were my way of illustrating what I believe is a new spiritual awareness sweeping humanity. In the adventures, I was trying to describe the personal revelations that each of us seems to be experiencing as our awareness increases. Written as stories, and based on my own experiences, these revelations could be easily portrayed within a specific plot and group of characters much like they were happening in the real world.

In this role, I've always thought of myself in terms of a journalist or social commentator, attempting to experientially document and illustrate particular changes in the human ethos that I believe are already occurring. In fact, I believe the evolution continues to move forward as the culture experiences ever more spiritual insight. At least two more novels in the Celestine series are planned.

I've chosen a nonfiction format for this book because I think, as human beings, we are in a very special place in relationship to this growing awareness. We all seem to glimpse it, even to live it for a time, and then, for reasons we will discuss in this book, we are often thrown off balance and have to struggle to regain our spiritual perspective. This book is about dealing with those challenges, and the key, I believe, lies in our ability to really discuss what we are experiencing with each other, and to do so as openly and as honestly as possible.

Fortunately, we seem to have passed an important landmark in this regard. Most of us now seem to be speaking about our spiritual experiences without undo self-consciousness and fear of criticism. Skeptics still abound, but the balance of opinion seems to have shifted, so that the knee-jerk ridicule of the past is no longer so common. We once tended to hide our syn-chronistic experiences from others, and even to dismiss them ourselves, for fear of being the subject of jokes and laughter. Now, in what seems like only a few short years, the scales have tipped in the other direction, and those who are too closed-minded are now taken to task for their skepticism.

Public opinion is shifting, I believe, because enough of us are aware that such extreme skepticism is nothing more than an old habit fashioned by centuries of adherence to the Newtonian-Cartesian view of the world. Sir Isaac Newton was a great physicist, but as many current thinkers have declared,[2] he shortchanged the universe by reducing it to a secular machine, describing it as operating only according to unwavering mechanistic laws. The seventeenth-century philosopher René Descartes preceded Newton by popularizing the idea that all we need to know about the universe is its basic laws, and that while these operations might have been first pushed into motion by a creator, they now function totally on their own.[3] After Newton and Descartes, any contention that there is an active spiritual force in the universe or that higher spiritual experience is anything other than hallucination was too often dismissed out of hand.

In this book, we will see that this old mechanistic worldview has been discredited since the early decades of the twentieth century, chiefly through the influence of Albert Einstein, the pioneers of quantum physics, and the newer research on prayer and intentionality. But the prejudices of the mechanistic worldview linger in our consciousness, guarded by an extreme skepticism that serves to screen out the more subtle spiritual perceptions that would challenge its assumptions.

Understanding how this works is important. In most cases, to experience higher spiritual experience, we must be at least open to the possibility that such perception exists. We know now that one actually has to suspend or "bracket" skepticism and try in every way possible to open up to spiritual phenomena in order to experience them. We must "knock on the door," as it has been expressed in Scripture, before any of these spiritual experiences can even be detected at all.

If we approach spiritual experience with a mind that is too closed and doubting, we perceive nothing and thereby prove to ourselves, quite erroneously and repeatedly, that higher spiritual experience is a myth. For centuries, we cast out these perceptions not because they weren't real, but because at the time, we didn't want them to be real. They didn't fit into our secular view of the world.

As we shall see in greater detail later, this skeptical attitude gained supremacy in the seventeenth century because the failing medieval worldview it succeeded was so full of contrived theories, charlatans on power trips, hexes and salvation for sale, and all manner of insanity. In this setting, thinking people longed for an established, scientific description of the physical universe that cut through all the nonsense. We wanted to see the world around us as reliable and natural. We wanted to be free of all the superstition and myth, and create a world where we could develop economic security—without thinking that strange and weird things were going to pop up in the dark to scare us. Because of this need, we understandably began the modern age with an overly materialistic and simplified view of the universe.

To say that we threw the baby out with the bathwater is an understatement. Life in modern times began to feel devoid of the inspiration that only higher spiritual meaning can provide. Even our religious institutions were affected. The miracles of religious mythology were too often reduced to metaphors, and churches became more about social togetherness, moral teaching, and intellectual belief than about the pursuit of actual spiritual experience.[4]

Yet, with our perception of synchronicity and other spiritual experiences in the current historical moment, we are connecting with a genuine spirituality that has always been our potential. In a sense, this awareness is not even new. It is the same kind of experience that some human beings have had throughout history, documented by a whole treasury of writers and artists around the world, including William James, Carl Jung, Thoreau and Emerson, Aldous Huxley (who called such knowing the Perennial Philosophy), and, in recent decades, George Leonard, Michael Murphy, Fritjof Capra, Marilyn Ferguson, and Larry Dossey.[5]

The scale on which these experiences are now entering human consciousness is, however, completely unprecedented. So many people are now having personal spiritual experiences that we are creating nothing less than a new worldview, one that includes and extends the old materialism and transforms it into something more advanced.

The social change we are talking about is not a revolution, where the structures of society are torn down and rebuilt as one ideology overcomes another. What is occurring now is an internal shift in which the individual changes first, and the institutions of human culture more or less look the same but are rejuvenated and transformed *in place,* because of a new outlook by those who maintain them.

As this transformation plays out, most of us will probably remain in the general line of work we have always pursued, in the families we love, and in the particular religions we find most truthful. But our vision of how our work and family and religious life should be lived and experienced will transform dramatically as we integrate and act on the higher experiences we perceive.

My observation—as I have expressed before—is that this transformation in awareness is sweeping across human culture through a kind of positive social contagion. Once enough people begin to live this awareness in an open way, discussing it freely, then others see this modeled awareness and immediately realize that it allows them to live outwardly more of what they already intuitively know inside. Afterward these others begin to emulate the new approach, eventually discovering those same experiences—and others—for themselves, and go on to be models in their own right.

This is the process of social evolution and consensus building in which we are all engaged in the waning years of the twentieth century. In this way, we are creating, I believe, a way of life that will ultimately drive the next century and millennium. The purpose of this book is to more directly explore the experiences so many of us are sharing, to review the history of our awakening, and to look closely at the specific challenges involved in living this way of life every day.

It is my hope that this work will confirm the underlying reality behind the information illustrated in the first two novels of the Celestine series, and, while far from complete, will help to further clarify our picture of the new spiritual awareness already forming out there.

—J.R.
Summer 1997

THE
CELESTINE
VISION

1

EARLY INTUITIONS

Our new spiritual awareness first began to emerge, I believe, in the late 1950s, when, at the very apex of modern materialism, something quite profound began to happen in our collective psyche. As if standing on the pinnacle of centuries of material accomplishment, we seemed to have paused and asked, "What now?" There seemed to be a mass intuition that something *more* was possible in human life, that some greater sense of fulfillment could be attained than our culture had been able to articulate and live.

The first thing we did with our intuition, of course, was to look at ourselves—or rather at the institutions and lifestyles we saw in the culture surrounding us—with a kind of restless criticism. As has been well chronicled, the emotional climate at the time was stiff and

1

class-oriented. Jews, Catholics, and women had a hard time attaining leadership positions. Blacks and other ethnic minorities were excluded completely. And the rest of affluent society suffered from a vast case of material judgmentalness.

With the meaning of life reduced to secular economics, status was achieved by how successful one appeared, creating all the hilarious efforts to keep up with the Joneses. Most of us were instilled with a terribly uptight *outer-directedness*, always judging ourselves according to what those around us might think. And we yearned for a society that could somehow liberate our potential.

THE SIXTIES

So we first asked *more* from our culture, which led to the many reform movements that characterized the 1960s. Quickly, there arose many legal initiatives seeking racial and gender equality, protection for the environment, even opposition to the disastrous undeclared war in Vietnam. We can see now that underneath the turmoil, the decade of the 1960s represented the first mass departure—the first "crack in the cosmic egg," as Joseph Chilton Pearce called it—in the dominant secular worldview.[1] Western culture, and to some extent human culture in general, was beginning to look past its materialistic orientation to search for a deeper philosophical meaning of life.

We began to sense, on a scale larger than ever, that our awareness and experience need not be limited by the narrow focus of the material age, that everyone ought to be functioning and interacting at a higher level. We knew at a level deeper than we could explain that we could somehow break out and become more creative and alive and free as human beings.

Unfortunately, our first actions reflected the competitive dramas of the day. Everybody looked at everyone else, and at the various institutions that irritated us, and demanded that the social structures reform. In essence, we looked around us at society and said to others, "You should change." While this activism certainly led to basic legal reforms that were helpful, it left untouched the more personal problems of insecurity, fear, and greed that have always been at the core of prejudice, inequality, and environmental damage.

THE SEVENTIES

By the time the 1970s arrived, we began to understand this problem. As we shall see later, the influence of the modern depth psychologists, the new humanistic approach to therapy, and the growing volume of self-help literature in the marketplace began to filter into the culture.[2] We realized that we were asking others to change but were missing the conflicts within ourselves. We began to see that if we were going to find the *more* we were looking for, we had to look past the behavior of others and look within. To change the world, we first had to change ourselves.

Almost overnight, going to a therapist lost its negative stigma, and it became acceptable, even trendy, to actively explore our inner psyches. We discovered that a review of our early family history, as the Freudians knew, often created a kind of insight or catharsis about our individual anxieties and defenses, and how and when these complexes originated in our childhood.[3]

Through this process, we could identify ways in which we were underactualized or holding ourselves back. Immediately, we realized that this focus within, this analysis of our personal history, was helpful and important. Yet, in the end, we found that something was still missing. We found we could analyze our inner psychology for years, only to have our same old fears and reactions and outbursts come back again every time we were in situations of high stress and insecurity.

By the end of the 1970s, we realized that our intuition of *more* could not be satisfied by therapy alone. What we were intuiting was a new awareness, a new sense of self, and a higher flow of experience that would replace the old habits and reactions that plagued us. The fuller life we sensed was not about mere psychological growth. The new awareness necessitated a deeper transformation that could only be called spiritual.

THE EIGHTIES AND NINETIES

In the 1980s, this insight seemed to take us in three directions. The first was marked by a return to the traditional religions. With a renewed spark of commitment, many of us engaged in a rereading of the scriptures and holy rituals of our heritage, looking for the answer to our intuition in a deeper consideration of the conventional spiritual pathways.

The second course seemed to be a more general and personal spiritual search that we directed ourselves, where we sought a closer understanding of the more esoteric spiritual pathways that had been found throughout history.

The third direction was a flight from idealism or spirituality altogether. Frustrated with the introspection of the sixties and seventies, many of us wanted to recapture the sleepy materialism of the fifties, where economic life alone seemed to suffice. If anything, however, this attempt to make economic reward a substitute for the higher-life meaning we intuited only led to an inner pressure to get rich quick. The excesses that typified the decade of the 1980s were exemplified by the savings-and-loan scandals and the many stock market corruptions.

I've always called the eighties a return to the Wild West, as the three urges—an attempted return to materialism and a renewed exploration of the spiritual both old and new—convulsed and competed. As we can see now in retrospect, all were attempts to find the something *more* that we felt was just around the corner. We experimented, pretended, competed for attention, raising much of what we did to the level of a superficial fad, and, in the end, we were left disappointed.

Yet I believe all that occurred in the 1980s was important, especially this first mass interest in various spiritual approaches. It was a necessary step that left us tired of the hype and commercialism and took us to a deeper level. In a way, it was a clearing that left us looking for real substance and convinced us finally that what we were looking for was a more profound shift in our attitudes and way of being.

In fact, I believe the collective intuition of the eighties took the form of one basic message: regardless of whether we are exploring the spirituality of our traditional religions or the experiences described by the mystics of a more esoteric path, there is a profound difference between knowing about and debating spiritual perception and actually experiencing these perceptions ourselves.

At the beginning of the nineties, then, we found ourselves in a very important place. If our sixties' intuition was correct, and a fuller life experience was possible, we knew clearly that we must move past a mere intellectual consideration and find the real experience. As a result, the hype and faddism died down, but the search for the real experience didn't. That's why our openness to spirituality has now reached a new level of authenticity and discussion.

LOOKING FOR THE REAL

It was in this setting that *The Celestine Prophecy, The Tenth Insight,* and a host of other books dealing with real spiritual perception were published and read by millions of people around the world. These books reached out to the mainstream precisely because they sought to describe our spiritual yearnings in real terms, pointing to experiences that were actually attainable.

In the 1960s, the prevailing idealism of the times had led me into a career working with emotionally challenged adolescents and their families, first as a caseload therapist and then as an administrator. Looking back on that work now, I can see a profound relationship between those experiences and the eventual creation of *Celestine.* Through working with these youths, all of whom had experienced severe early abuse, I began to see the larger picture of what they were having to overcome. To heal what had happened to them, they had to embark on a particular journey that in some sense had to include the transcendent.

The anxiety of early abuse creates a severe need in children to take control of life. They fashion dramas, sometimes severe and self-destructive ones, in order to give themselves a sense of meaning and hence reduce their anxiety. Breaking the pattern of these dramas can be extremely difficult, but therapists have found success by facilitating the perception of peak moments of success with athletics, group interactions, meditation, and other activities. These activities are designed to promote the experience of a higher self to replace the old identity and its attendant reaction pattern.

To some extent, each of us is hit one way or another with the same kind of anxiety abused children experience. In most cases, thankfully, this anxiety is of a lesser degree, and our reaction patterns are not as extreme, but the process, the growth step involved, is exactly the same. This realization, as I watched it play out in my work, clarified in my mind what the whole culture seemed to be going through. We knew that life-as-usual seemed to be missing something that could be attained through an inner transformative experience, a real change in how we perceive ourselves and life that produces a higher, more spiritual personal identity. The effort to describe this psychological journey became the basis of *The Celestine Prophecy*.

CELESTINE

The actual writing of *The Celestine Prophecy* occurred from January 1989 through April 1991 and was characterized by a sort of trial-and-error process. Quite amazingly, as I remembered earlier experiences and wrote about them, lacing them into an adventure tale, striking coincidences would occur to emphasize the particular points that I wanted to make. Books would show up mysteriously, or I would have timely encounters with the exact sort of individuals I was attempting to describe. Sometimes strangers would open up to me for no apparent reason and tell me about their spiritual experiences. Compelled to give them the manuscript, I found that their reactions to it always suggested the need for revision or expansion.

The signal that the book was near completion came when many of these people began to ask for copies of the manuscript for friends. My first search for a publisher met with no success, and I hit what was the first of what I think of now as brick walls. All the coincidences stopped and I felt dead in the water. At this point, I finally began to apply what I think is one of the most important truths of the new awareness. This was an attitude I knew of and had experienced before, but it was not yet integrated thoroughly enough into my consciousness to access in a stressful situation.

I was interpreting the complete lack of publishing opportunities as a failure, a negative event, and that was the interpretation that had stopped the coincidences that I felt had been leading me forward. When I realized what was happening, I snapped to attention and made more revisions in the book, emphasizing this point. And in my own life, I knew I had to treat this development as I would any other event. What was its meaning? Where was the message?

Within days, a friend mentioned that she had met an individual who had recently moved to our area from New York, where he had worked in publishing for many years. Immediately, I saw an image in my mind of myself going to see him, and the intuition had a deep feeling of inspiration about it. The next day I was there, and the coincidences took off again. He now wanted to work with individuals who were planning to self-publish, he told me, and since my manuscript was getting a high number of word-of-mouth referrals, he felt this approach could be successful.

Shortly afterward we were again ready to go to print, and I had met Salle Merrill, who brought with her a sensitive female perspective and a timely emphasis on the importance of giving. Of the first three thousand copies of the book we printed, we mailed or personally gave away fifteen hundred to small bookshops and individuals in Alabama, Florida, North Carolina, and Virginia. Word-of-mouth recommendations by the first readers took care of everything else.

In six months, the book had over 100,000 copies in print, was in all fifty states, and was appearing in countries around the world. It sold so many copies so quickly, not because of any publicity I did, but because others also began to give it away to their friends everywhere.

PURSUING OUR DREAMS

I mention the above story to illustrate that our new spiritual awareness is all about actualizing dreams, an experience that has always been at the heart of human striving everywhere. The universe truly seems to be set up as a platform for the actualization of our deepest and most heartfelt aspirations. It is a dynamic system propelled by nothing less than the constant flow of small miracles. But there is a catch. The universe is built to respond to our consciousness, but it will give back to us only the level of quality that we put in. Therefore, the process of discovering who we are and what we are here to do and of learning to follow the mysterious coincidences that can guide us is dependent, to a great extent, on our ability to stay positive and to find the silver lining in all events.

Living the new spiritual awareness is a matter of passing through a series of steps or revelations. Each step broadens our perspective. But each step also presents its own set of challenges. It is not enough to merely glimpse each level of expanded awareness. We must intend to live it, to integrate each increased degree of awareness into our daily routine. It only takes one negative interpretation to stop everything.

In the pages that follow, we will examine these steps not just in terms of inner experience but from the perspective of holding them firm in our lives and putting them into effective practice.

2

EXPERIENCING THE
COINCIDENCES

Meaningful coincidences can happen at any moment. We may be going through our day when, seemingly without warning, an odd chance occurrence grabs our attention. We may think of an old friend who hasn't crossed our mind for years; then, after totally forgetting about it, we run into this person the next day. Similarly, we may see an individual at work that we think we might like to know, only to find that very individual sitting across from us at a restaurant later that day.

Coincidences can involve the timely arrival of some special information that we want but have no idea how to get, or the sudden realization that our experience with a past hobby or interest was actually a preparation for landing us a new opportunity or job. Regardless of the details of a particular coincidence, we sense that it is too unlikely to have been the result of luck or mere chance. When a coincidence grabs our attention, we are held, even if only for a moment, in awe of the occurrence. At some level, we sense that such events were destined in some way, that they were *supposed* to happen just when they did in order to shift our lives in a new, more inspiring direction.

Abraham Lincoln wrote of one such coincidence that happened in his youth. At that time, Lincoln felt that he was to do more with his life than be a farmer or craftsman like the other residents of his Illinois community. One day he encountered a peddler who had obviously fallen on hard times and who asked Lincoln to buy an old barrel of goods, mostly worthless, for a dollar. Lincoln could have easily brushed off the failed merchant, but he gave the peddler the money and stored the goods. Only later, when he cleaned out the barrel, did Lincoln find among the old cans and utensils a full set of lawbooks, with which he studied to become a lawyer and went on to pursue his remarkable destiny.[1]

The Swiss psychologist Carl Jung was the first modern thinker to define this mysterious phenomenon. He called it *synchronicity,* the perception of meaningful coincidence. Jung maintained that synchronicity was an acausal principle in the universe, a law that operated to move human beings toward greater growth in consciousness.[2]

Jung witnessed a prime example of synchronicity

during one of his therapy sessions. His patient was a particularly proper lady who was having problems with her obsessive behavior. Jung was exploring her dreams, hoping to help her get in touch with the light, playful, and intuitive side of her nature. Her most recent dreams involved an interaction with a scarab beetle, but she was adamantly resisting all attempts at interpretation. Just at that moment, Jung heard a strange tapping on the window, and when he opened the drapes, there on the outside of the window sat a scarab, an insect that was very rare in that area. The episode so inspired the woman that, according to Jung, she went on to make great advances in the treatment of her condition.[3]

Few of us can look back at our lives and not see a pattern of synchronicity in the mysterious events that transpired to bring us our current career, our spouse, or the network of friends and alliances on which we rely. Much more difficult is the perception of such important life events in the present, as they happen. Coincidences can be dramatic, as we've seen. But they can also be very subtle and fleeting, and thus easily dismissed—as the old material worldview would have us do—as mere chance or happenstance.

Our personal challenge is to overcome the cultural conditioning that leads us to reduce life to the ordinary, commonplace, and nonmysterious. Most of us have learned to pursue life with our egos alone, waking up in the morning and thinking we must take complete control of our day. We create inflexible mental lists of projects we intend to accomplish, and pursue these ends with a kind of tunnel vision. Yet the mystery is always there, dancing around the fringe of our lives, giving us fleeting glimpses of possibility. We must decide to slow down and shift our focus, and begin to act on the opportunities coming our way.

NIGHT DREAMS

Of all the synchronistic experiences we can have, night dreams are perhaps the most nebulous and hard to interpret. Yet our culture has always been fascinated with these nighttime encounters. They are the stuff of mythology and prophecy, and at some level we know they are relevant to our lives. But how?

Usually, dreams are stories, although they often take the form of nonsensical plots and weird characters, placing together people and scenes in ways that couldn't possibly occur in real life. For this reason, most of us quickly lose interest in trying to interpret them. The images are too difficult, so we dismiss the jumble of scenes as practically useless and go on with our day.

But the experts who work with dreams would caution us not to give up too soon.[4] They tell us that dreams have important meanings lying hidden in the symbolism. A simple perusal of the many dream books on the market can give one an overview of dream symbolism, which is the mythological or archetypal meanings that can be assigned to the various elements in dreams, from animals to acts of murder, flight, or stealing.

Yet I believe the key to discovering the synchronicity of dreams is to ultimately go beyond the standard interpretation of these symbols and focus on the larger picture: the meaning surrounding the plot and characters of the dream. Here we can find messages of a more personal nature that often pertain directly to the specific situations we face in our lives.

For example, if we dream of ourselves in a war of some kind, fleeing a battle, and then, as the dream develops, we discover some way not only to survive but to help end the fighting, this theme may apply to our own real-life situation. Obviously, we aren't really in a war, but what about other kinds of conflict that the war may be symbolizing in our own lives? Are we fleeing? Or avoiding the confrontation by hiding or denying or distracting ourselves with other things, hoping the problem will go away?

The key to understanding the dream's message is to compare the basic plot of the dream—in this case running from war (conflict) yet later finding a solution—with the real situation in our individual world. Perhaps this dream is telling us to wake up and see the conflict and know that a potential solution can be found if we pay attention.

And what about the characters in the dream? Although the characters may be strange, we must ask how they might symbolize real people with whom we are currently having important interactions. Are we seeing the people in our lives accurately? Perhaps the dream is telling us something about who these people really are, for better or worse.

But what if we analyze the plot and characters of the dream and find absolutely no connection with our situation at all? What do we do? Here it is important to write down the dream in a journal, because the dream may be prophetic. It is easy to think that prophetic dreams are only those with dramatic results, having to do with avoiding plane crashes or inheriting a fortune from a forgotten relative. But in reality, dreams that focus on smaller everyday problems can also be prophetic. Often the reason dreams seem bizarre and silly is that the situation they describe has not yet occurred in our lives. Instead of dismissing it, we are served better by keeping it in mind. It could be amazingly instructive later.

SEEING OR THINKING OF AN OLD FRIEND

The synchronicity of seeing or thinking of an old friend is usually more straightforward. If it begins with a thought, the image usually just pops into our minds without association to another event. We might even comment to ourselves on how long it has been since we last thought of or talked with this person. Very often this happens early in the morning, in that quiet time between being asleep and waking.

Unfortunately, our cultural habit is to linger only so long with these images and then to dismiss them in order to go on with our day. This tendency can lead us to miss the greater meaning of the memory. But if we pay close attention to such thoughts, other synchronistic events might also begin to occur. We might be looking for something else and run into a second reminder of the person we had thought of—perhaps an old photograph or letter that evokes more memories of events shared with that person. Upon reflection, we might even find that these same circumstances are coming up again in our present lives.

Of course, other synchronicities might occur as well. We may be walking down the street and look up to see that very individual walking toward us. Or we might answer the phone to discover the person on the other end of the line.

Our challenge is to always follow up on these coincidences. If we can't talk with the old friend right at the moment, we can make a later date for lunch or tea. There is always important information needing to be exchanged. If it is not about old situations that need to be revisited and cleared, it will be about something new that we or our old friends have discovered and need to convey to each other. The key is to pursue the mystery, to look beneath the surface, to explore.

Sometimes, after spontaneously thinking of someone, we will want to take the initiative ourselves and call him or her immediately. I've often had the experience of reaching for the phone to call an old friend and having it ring before I can pick it up because the friend was calling me. Once again, the key is to talk about what is happening with the other person and ourselves, describing our specific life situations at the moment, searching for the instructive message that explains the reason the coincidence has occurred.

CHANCE MEETINGS

Another type of synchronicity is the purely chance meeting, which can involve friends, acquaintances, or total strangers. In the case of someone we know, we will find ourselves running across this person in a way that is beyond what we would expect by pure chance.

Running into an old friend at a critical time is one such example. Deepak Chopra, a leading advocate of the new mind/body medicine, talks about a series of experiences that first led him to seriously consider alternative medical approaches. Up until that time, he had practiced medicine as a traditional Western M.D. and held prestigious positions at Harvard and other universities as a professor of immunology.

Then his life began to change. During a trip to deliver a lecture, he was invited to visit with an Eastern leader of meditation, who suggested he study Ayurvedic medicine, an Eastern approach that focuses on the prevention of disease. Deepak dismissed the idea, wanting nothing to do with any approach that sounded mystical.

After the meeting, he drove to the airport, where to his surprise he ran into an old friend from medical school. In the course of their conversation, this friend pulled out a copy of the basic text of Ayurvedic medicine and commented that he thought Chopra would find it interesting. Overwhelmed by the coincidence, Deepak read the book, recognized that to champion this medical approach was his destiny, and went on to pursue his career of popularizing alternative medicine around the world.[5]

Another synchronicity of this type occurs when we repeatedly see someone we don't know within a short period of time. The odds against such occurrences are tremendous, but they seem to happen quite frequently. We see a person once and usually think nothing of it. But when we see the same individual again, or even a third time in the same day, the coincidence usually gets our attention. Unfortunately, too often we simply note the event, thinking it odd, and then go on our way, taking no action.

Again, the challenge is to find a way to pursue a conversation with this individual. This is difficult enough when we know the person, but it becomes harder when it involves a stranger. First of all, there is the problem of the defensive posture most of us take toward strangers. In Western cultures, eye contact and initiating conversation have too often been construed as an invasion of privacy or even sexual overture. It is an unfortunate assumption in our society, for instance, that if a woman makes eye contact with a man, she is sending a signal that she is open to his sexual advances. This creates all kinds of confusion—women often averting their eyes when going down the street, for fear that an aggressive male will make assumptions, or men, sensitive to the problem, not even trying to make direct eye contact with women for fear of being labeled aggressive.

While this remains a problem, our intuitions, thankfully, usually don't let us down in this respect. If we pay attention, and learn to perceive the energy flow, we will know whom we should open up to and whom we should shy away from. It is equally important to consciously analyze the appropriateness of our own sexual energy in this regard.

I believe we are finding that proceeding in an intentionally friendly manner always works best. We can say something specific such as "Didn't I see you before?" and follow up with a description of our specific life situation. If we happen to be in a store, we might say, "I'm here to buy clothes for a party coming up." Hopefully, the other person will respond by saying why she is in the store and we will discover a common life theme. Remember, the goal is to discern the reason for the synchronicity.

Older people seem to be much better with this kind of spontaneous conversation, but all of us can break through our sense of awkwardness if our intent is very sincere. In any case, all we can do is try, and if we are rejected, take it in good humor. As my grandfather once said, "The secret of life is learning to make a fool of yourself gracefully." Obviously, we should always take precautions when getting to know strangers (meeting only in public places until we get to know them, for instance). But if we proceed appropriately, the rewards can be a richer flow of synchronicity.

INFORMATION ARRIVING AT JUST THE RIGHT MOMENT

Another important synchronistic event is the experience of having information we need come to us at just the right time. This experience sometimes begins with a sudden heightened sense of expectation. We could be anywhere, in a work situation or at leisure, when we begin to feel as though something important is about to happen. As we will explore later, occasionally we experience a perception of lightness in our bodies or the sense of everything around us becoming brighter and more luminous. Something tells us our lives are about to shift in some important direction.

How the information arrives is always a mystery.

Usually, it comes to us through another human being, either in her words or through her actions. It can also come in the form of a book, magazine, or news item. But it is always a human being's perspective, research, or idea about the world that comes to us just at the right moment to expand our own awareness.

Our sense that the information is coming is probably the result of our having integrated all the growth steps necessary to set up our readiness for the next chapter in our life story. I had an experience like this involving my understanding of human power struggles. Up until that point, I had grasped clearly that human beings competed with each other in irrational ways, but I knew that there was more about power struggles that could be understood. At a certain point, I had the expectation that I was about to experience a leap forward.

For a while, nothing occurred. Then I was out driving one day, and I realized that a particular bookstore had captured my eye. I pulled in and began to browse, my sense of anticipation increasing. At just that moment, from at least thirty feet away, a book jumped out at me. Even at that distance, its color and graphics seemed distinct from all the other books stacked around it. I immediately rushed over to find Ernest Becker's *Escape from Evil,* a book that outlines the way humans tend to build themselves up at other people's expense in order to feel more secure and to gain a greater sense of self-esteem and well-being.[6] This was the key step in my understanding of power struggles that had been missing.

In summary, the most important keys in learning to take advantage of the various synchronicities in our lives are to stay alert and to make the time necessary to explore what is occurring. In order to do this, each of us needs to create in our life a sufficient amount of what I call drift time—time where we are doing nothing but hanging out, clicking through stations on television, flipping through the newspaper, or walking down the street alert to the world around us. If you think of a friend, drop by; see what happens. The Internet is also an interesting source of information in this regard. We must remember, however, that anyone can put anything on the Internet. There's no editor or fact-checker to assure accuracy and no publisher to hold responsible for content.

RELATING SYNCHRONICITY TO OUR RELIGIOUS BELIEFS

For some, relating an ongoing perception of synchronicity to our religious beliefs is a challenge. Yet I think, in most cases, there is no conflict. As we begin to perceive the coincidences in our lives, the mystery brings us face-to-face with the deeper spiritual questions of life. What is this force that seems to be pulling us toward our destiny? Is there a divine purpose for our lives? How is this purpose revealed to us, exactly?

Most of us grow up with at least an idea of religious tradition. If we are not committed to a particular religious perspective ourselves, we have close friends or relatives who are, and who deeply believe in the tenets of their faiths. I firmly believe that most people who are committed in this way to a particular religion are acting on an honest inner drive to keep its unique contributions alive in the world. This common impulse guarantees the larger human society a wide diversity of religious beliefs through which we can explore many options and thus grow. In my opinion, each positive religious perspective contains an important part of the truth. The general dialogue between the various religions, as vague and fragmented as it is, nonetheless is critical to our ongoing evolution toward a better overall spiritual understanding.

Our perception of synchronicity in itself does not suggest that any one religious tradition is more advantageous than another. Synchronicity, as well as the overall new spiritual awareness that we're building, is merely a consciousness of the way the divine operates in our lives. All major religions—Hindu, Buddhist, Jewish, Christian, Islamic—as well as many shamanic traditions share the notion of being responsive to the will of God. To put it differently, all are concerned with our growth toward unity with a Godhead or coming into communion with the creative force behind the human condition. Our new awareness of synchronicity is just the perception or experience of our connection with this divine force.

I can remember wondering about this question of doing God's will as a young child growing up in a rural Protestant church. There was no doubt in my mind, even then, that this particular church and the surrounding community were special. Community support and loving interaction still led to barn raisings and a quick response to sickness in a member's family. The Protestant Christianity the members practiced was surprisingly open and nonjudgmental for that time.

Central to this particular church's theology was the conversion experience, the acceptance of Christianity. But the implicit assumption was that afterward one had to discover and then follow God's will for one's own life. As a child I was frustrated because no one ever discussed in detail how one might go about finding and following God's will. Of course, this was at a time when society was at the height of its secular, materialistic attitude. Yet I was full of questions: What is the nature of this God with whom we must commune? How is the divine presence really experienced? What does being in alignment with divine intention really feel like? To these questions, the other church members had no answers. But the look on their faces made me realize that they knew; they just had no words with which to express it.

I think that it is part of our new spiritual awareness now to answer more of these questions consciously. For centuries, corrupt medieval churchmen used fear and ignorance to charge money for blessings and salvation, discouraging any kind of advanced spiritual perception on the part of their constituency. And a few do the same thing today. But for the most part, I believe we are collectively realizing the importance of shared spiritual awareness and discussion. More and more of us in organized religions are realizing that our perception of synchronicity represents an extension and clarification of the best of our religious traditions. This perception is direct evidence of a divine force active in our lives, a divine force that our intuition and faith have always told us was there.

RESPONDING TO SKEPTICISM

Perhaps the biggest challenge to those of us beginning to live the new spiritual awareness is relating to skeptics. All of us, once we open up to the reality of synchronicity, find ourselves at times talking to someone who reacts negatively to our beliefs and directly questions the validity of our experiences. Although the skeptics are shrinking in number, there are still plenty of adherents to the old materialistic worldview who consider conversations about the mystical fanciful and unfounded. These discussions directly threaten their commonsense beliefs about what is real and rational in the natural world.

The skeptics we run into seem to fall into two broad categories. The largest group is those who take a skeptical position not because they have thoroughly investigated the wide range of mystical encounters they are hearing about, but because they haven't. They don't have the time or inclination to look into such experiences, so they adopt the stance on the subject that feels safest: labeling it all absurd. Usually, these skeptics live and work among lots of doubters, who are critical of any new creation or assertion and who use ridicule as a means of gaining personal power over others. In that kind of environment, most people adopt a strictly conventional position to avoid conflict.

The other type of skeptic we run into is the true adherent to scientific materialism. This is a person who might research to some extent the arena of mystical experience but who always falls back to the barricades of materialism, demanding objective proof of such claims. Arguments that mystical experiences have a consistent character over long historical periods or that thousands of unrelated people report the same thing or that statistical studies have repeatedly shown that intuitive and psychic ability is a natural occurrence, all fall on deaf ears.

In dealing with skeptics, several approaches have proved to be effective. First of all, we must remember that a degree of skepticism is, in fact, important. All of us must avoid taking a faddish idea at face value and must look at any assertion about the nature of reality with a critical eye.

Yet we must not forget that there is an equally important corollary to this principle, one that is too often forgotten: to stay open-minded enough to consider the phenomenon in question. Maintaining this balance between skepticism and openness is especially difficult when the phenomenon involves our inner psychology or spirituality.

Two other important points are to always keep conversations friendly and to push toward areas of agreement. I would venture that almost everyone who now experiences perceptions of a mystical or spiritual nature was an extreme skeptic at one point in the past. In this sense, we are all ex-skeptics, and it may be important to remind ourselves again that the process of opening up to the mystical side of life is happening mainly through personal interaction; we see another taking seriously the idea of spiritual experience, and afterward we decide to investigate the matter ourselves.

For this reason, we must take every conversation seriously. Our frank disclosure just might be the testimony that breaks a person's entrenched position. And guess what? The reverse might also be true: the skeptic we're speaking to might be correct on a given issue. Those of us who are exploring the potentials of human experience are doing nothing if we're not committed to a two-way process of consensus building. We all have to listen

to learn. It is open dialogue that ensures a widely debated viewpoint and keeps our perspective broad.

TAKING SYNCHRONICITY
SERIOUSLY

Glimpsing the coincidences, then, and beginning a dialogue about them openly without falling into negative
interpretations are the first steps in living our new spiritual awareness. Yet it does not take long for more questions to come. If the synchronicity we perceive is
evidence of the operation of a spiritual force in our lives,
why have we in Western culture ignored these mysterious events for so long? And why is an awareness of synchronicity surfacing now, at this moment in time? What
is the larger historical picture of what is happening to
us?

These are the questions that take us to the next level
of awareness.

3

UNDERSTANDING
WHERE WE ARE

When we get up in the morning and look out our windows, we see the modern world beginning to awaken for the day. Neighbors leave their homes and drive away in their cars for the morning commute to work. Overhead, perhaps, we hear the drone of a plane. A delivery truck full of mass-produced goods rolls by to restock the supersized grocery store down the street.

For some of us, the long story of history that ends in this moment of observation is merely a litany of economic and technological progress. But for more of us every day, history is becoming a more psychological question. How did we come to live like this? How was our everyday reality shaped and formed by those who came before us? Why do we believe what we believe?

History, of course, is the larger context of our individual lives. Without it, we live only in the superficial and provincial reality we inherited as children. An accurate understanding of history gives our awareness of the world depth and substance. It hovers around all that we see like a frame of meaning that tells us who we are and gives us a reference point for where we seem to be heading.

REPLACING THE MEDIEVAL COSMOLOGY

The story of our modern, largely Western way of looking at the world begins at least five hundred years ago with the collapse of the medieval worldview. As is well known, this old world was characterized and maintained by the central authority of the early Christian church. The church, of course, was largely responsible for rescuing Western civilization from total disintegration after the fall of Rome, but in so doing, the churchmen took upon themselves a great power, defining the purposes of life in Christendom for a millennium based around their interpretations of the Bible.

It is difficult to imagine just how little we humans knew in the Middle Ages about the physical processes of nature. We had little knowledge of the organs of the body or the biology of plant growth. Thunderstorms were believed to come from angry gods or the designs of the evil spirits. Nature and human life were cast in strictly religious terms. As Ernest Becker discusses in *The Structure of Evil,*[1] the medieval cosmology placed the earth at the very center of the universe as a great religious theater, which had been created for one great purpose: as the stage on which humankind either won or lost salvation. Everything—the weather, famine, the ravages of disease and war—was created strictly to test one's faith. And there to orchestrate the symphony of temptation was Satan. He was there, the churchmen said, to deceive our minds, foil our work, take advantage of our weaknesses, and spoil our bid for eternal happiness.

For those who were truly saved, eternity would be spent in the bliss of heaven. For those who failed, who succumbed to the temptations, fate would bring damnation in the lakes of fire—unless, of course, the churchmen intervened. The individuals of that day, facing such a reality, could not go directly to God to seek forgiveness, or even accurately assess whether they were passing this spiritual test, for the churchmen set themselves up as the sole gatekeepers to the divine and worked tirelessly to prevent the masses from having direct access to any holy texts. If they aspired to eternity in heaven, medieval citizens had no choice but to follow the often complicated and capricious dictates of the powerful church leaders.

The reasons for the collapse of this worldview are numerous. Expanding trade brought word of new cultures and outlooks that threw the medieval cosmology into question. The excesses and extremes of the churchmen eventually undermined the church's credibility. The invention of the printing press and distribution among the populations of Europe of both the Bible and the books of antiquity provided information directly to the masses, which in turn led to the Protestant revolution.[2]

A new line of thinkers—Copernicus and Galileo and Kepler—directly challenged the church's dogma concerning the structure of the solar system, the mathematics behind the orbits of the planets, and even mankind's place in the universe.[3] Over time, the belief that the earth lay at the center of the universe was thrown into doubt. And as the Renaissance and the Enlightenment emerged, God was pushed further and further from everyday consciousness.

THE ANXIETY OF LOSTNESS

Here we can see one of the important historical turning points in the formation of the modern worldview. The medieval worldview, as corrupt as it was, at least defined the whole of existence. It was an agreed-upon philosophy that was broad and comprehensive. It established meaning for the complete range of life events, including the reason for our existence and the criteria for entering a pleasant, heavenly plane after death. Life was explained in all its dimensions.

When the medieval cosmology began to collapse, we humans in the West were thrown into deep confusion concerning the higher existential meaning of our lives. If the churchmen were wrong, and untrustworthy, what was the true situation of humankind on this planet?

We looked around and realized that in the final analysis, we merely found ourselves here, whirling through space on a planet that circles one of a billion other stars, without knowing why. Surely, there was some God, some force of creation, that put us here for an intended purpose. But now we were surrounded by doubt and uncertainty, immersed in the angst of meaninglessness. How could we find the courage to live without having a clear idea of higher purpose? By the sixteenth century, Western culture was completely in transition; we were a people stuck in a no-man's-land between worldviews.

THE EMERGENCE OF SCIENCE

Eventually, we thought of a solution for our dilemma: science. We humans might be philosophically lost, but we realized that we could embrace a system through which we could find ourselves again. And this time we believed it would be a true knowledge, one free of the superstition and dogma that characterized the medieval world.

As a culture, we decided to launch a massive inquiry, an organized system of consensus making, to discover the facts of our real situation on this planet. We would empower science and mandate that it go out into this unknown place (the vast natural world, remember, had not even been named, much less explained at that time) to discover what was going on, and explain it to the people.

Our enthusiasm was so high that we felt that the scientific method could, in fact, even discover the real nature of God, the creative process lying at the heart of the universe. Science could, we believed, marshal the information necessary to give us back the sense of certainty and meaning that we had lost with the collapse of the old cosmology.

But the faith we had in a speedy discovery of our true human situation soon proved to be misplaced. To begin with, the church succeeded in pressuring science to focus only on the material world. Many of the early thinkers, including Galileo, were condemned or killed outright by the churchmen. As the Renaissance progressed, an unsteady truce developed. The wounded but still powerful church stubbornly claimed sole providence over the mental and spiritual lives of human beings. Only begrudgingly did it sanction scientific inquiry at all, and the churchmen insisted that science be applied only to the physical universe: the phenomena of stars, orbits, earth, plants, and our bodies.

Thankful for the territory, science began to focus on this physical world and quickly flourished. We began to map out the physics behind matter, our geological history, and the dynamics of the weather. The parts of the human body were named and the chemical operations of biological life were investigated. Careful not to pursue any of the implications its discoveries might hold for religion, science began to exclusively explore our outer world.

A MATERIALISTIC UNIVERSE

The first broad scientific picture about how this outer world operated was created by Sir Isaac Newton, who pulled together the views of the early astronomers into a model of the universe as stable and predictable. The mathematics of Newton suggested that the larger world operated according to unchanging natural laws, laws that could be counted on and used in practical ways.

Descartes had already made the case that the universe in its entirety—the orbiting of the earth and other planets around the sun, the circulation of the atmosphere as weather patterns, the interdependency of animal and plant species—all worked together like one great cosmic machine, or clockworks, always reliable and totally devoid of mystical influence.[4]

Newton's mathematics seemed to prove it so. And once this holistic picture was established in physics, everyone believed that the other disciplines of science had merely to fill in the details, discover the mini-processes, the smaller levers and springs that made the great clock run. As this began to occur, science became more and more specialized in its approach to mapping out the physical universe, dividing into ever smaller subdivisions and going into greater detail in naming and explaining the world around us.

Cartesian dualism and Newtonian physics established a philosophical position that was quickly embraced as the reigning worldview for the modern age. This view further advocated an empirical skepticism in which nothing about the universe should be believed unless it was shown by quantitative experiment to exist without question.

Following Francis Bacon, science became ever more secular and pragmatic in its orientation and moved further and further away from the deeper issues of mankind's spiritual life and purpose. If pressed, scientists would refer to a deistic notion of God, a deity that first pushed the universe into operation, leaving it ever afterward to operate totally by mechanical means.

THE ENLIGHTENMENT
SOLUTION

We come now to another key turning point in the formation of the modern worldview. We had turned to science to discover the answers to our largest existential and spiritual questions, but science became consumed with a purely secular and material focus. Who could tell how long it would take to discover the higher meaning of human life?

Clearly, we in the West needed a new banner of meaning, a new mind-set that we could hold on to in the meantime—and more important, one that would occupy our minds. And in this moment, the collective decision seemed to be to turn our attention to the physical world completely, just as science was doing. After all, science was discovering a rich bounty of natural resources, there for the taking. And we could use these resources to improve our economic situation, to make ourselves more comfortable in this secular world of ours. We might have to wait for knowledge about our true spiritual situation, but we could make ourselves more materially secure while we were waiting. Our new philosophy, albeit temporary, was a furtherance of human progress, a commitment to bettering our lives and the lives of our children.

At the very least, this new philosophy eased our minds. The sheer weight of the work to be done kept us busy, just as it kept our attention off the fact that the mystery of death, and thus of life itself, still loomed large and unexplained. Someday, at the end of our earthly existence, we would have to face the spiritual realities, whatever they were. In the meantime, however, we narrowed our focus to the problems of everyday material existence and tried to make progress itself, personal and collective, the sole reason for our short lives. And that became our psychological stance at the beginning of the modern age.

We only have to take a quick look around at the end of the twentieth century to see the grand results of this narrow focus on material progress. In a few centuries, we explored the world, founded nations, and created a huge global system of commerce. In addition, our science has conquered diseases, developed awesome forms of communication, and sent men to the moon.

Yet all this has been accomplished at great cost. Citing progress, we have exploited the natural environment almost to the level of destruction. And personally, we can see that at a certain point our focus on the economic aspects of life became an obsession used to push away the anxiety of uncertainty. We had made secular life and progress, ruled by our logic, the sole reality we would allow into our minds.

Western culture finally began to awaken from this preoccupation in the mid-twentieth century. We stopped and looked around and began to understand where we were in history. Ernest Becker won a Pulitzer Prize for his book *The Denial of Death*[5] because he clearly showed what the modern world had done to itself psychologically. We had narrowed our focus to material economics and for so long refused to entertain the idea of a deeper spiritual experience because we didn't want to be reminded of the great mystery that is this life.

I believe that's why old people tended to be abandoned in nursing homes. Looking at them reminded us of what we had pushed out of our consciousness. Our need to hide from the mystery that terrified us is also why a belief in a universe where synchronicity and other intuitive abilities are real has felt so foreign to our common sense. Our fear explains why, for so many years, those individuals who were experiencing mysterious synchronicity, intuition, prophetic dreams, ESP, near-death experiences, angelic contact, and all the rest— experiences that have always occurred in human existence, and even continued in the modern age—were met with so much skepticism. Talking about these experiences or even admitting that they were possible threatened our assumption that the secular world was all there was.

LIVING THE LONGER NOW

We can see, then, how our perception of the synchronicity in our lives represents nothing less than a collective awakening from a secular worldview that has lasted for centuries. Now when we look out on modern existence with its technological marvels, we can see this world from a more revealing psychological vantage point.

At the fall of the medieval age, we lost our sense of certainty about who we were and what our existence meant. So we invented a scientific method of inquiry and sent this system out to find the truth of our situation. But science seemed to splinter into a thousand faces, unable to immediately bring back a coherent picture.

In response, we pushed away our anxiety by turning our focus to practical endeavors, reduced life to its economic aspects only, and finally entered a collective obsession with the practical, material aspects of life. As we have seen, scientists set up a worldview that reinforced this obsession and for many centuries became lost in it themselves. The cost of this limited cosmology was the narrowing of human experience and the repression of our higher spiritual perception—a repression we are finally breaking through now.

Our challenge is to hold this perspective on history in our awareness, as a matter of practice, especially when the still-influential materialism reaches out to lull us back into the old view. We must remember where we are, the truth of the modern age, and make it part of every moment—for it is from this larger sense of aliveness that we can open up to the next step in our journey.

We can see, once we look with fresh eyes, that science has not completely failed us. There has always been an underlying current in science that was silently moving past the material obsession. Beginning in the first decades of the twentieth century, a new wave of thinking began to fashion a more complete description of the universe and of ourselves—a description that is finally making its way into popular consciousness.

4

ENTERING THE
RESPONSIVE
UNIVERSE

One of the most important landmarks in the emergence of a new scientific view of mankind and the universe is the work of Thomas Kuhn, who published *The Structure of Scientific Revolutions* in 1957.[1] This book first alerted us to the tendency of science to be selective in the way its practitioners both choose their own research and judge the work of others.

Kuhn convincingly showed that what he called *paradigm thinking* often led scientists to exclude areas of research, including particular findings that didn't easily fit in with the prevailing theories or constructs of the day. A paradigm is a set of beliefs about reality that seem self-evident and unchangeable. Paradigm thinking can lead individuals (in this case, scientists) to defend their viewpoint against rational evidence. This is exactly what occurred in the blind allegiance to the Newtonian paradigm. Kuhn's thesis also illuminated the problem of personal *investment* in science, revealing the way scientists often make their careers from particular discoveries, usually at universities or private institutes, and then tend to defend these theoretical positions—seeing them as the source of their personal status—against newcomers with different ideas, even if these ideas are objectively better and more complete.

Because of this problem, science often proceeds very slowly, with one generation having to retire before the next generation can have its accomplishments accepted. Kuhn's great contribution was in creating greater self-awareness and openness among a new generation of scientists, just when the popular realization arrived that a major paradigm shift was already under way.

Newton imaged the world as operating by purely physical processes of a machinelike nature, without mental or mystical influence of any kind. By following this paradigm, all the other sciences and subdisciplines had set out to label and explain all the parts and basic processes of the world.

However, at the end of the nineteenth century, at the very height of the mechanistic paradigm, the basic assumptions in physics that created this kind of science were being thrown into question. Suddenly, instead of being a dead, soulless place, the universe was beginning to look like a huge arena of dynamic, mysterious energy—an energy that underlay all things and interacted with itself in a manner that could only be called *intelligent*.

THE NEW PHYSICS

This shift toward a belief in the universe as intelligent began with the work of Albert Einstein, who in the course of several decades turned physics on its head. As Fritjof Capra has detailed in *The Tao of Physics*, Einstein burst on the scene when scientists were having difficulty understanding particular experimental data in the old way. The behavior of light, for instance, did not seem to fit easily into the Newtonian mechanistic view.[2]

Maxwell and Faraday had shown in 1860 that light could best be described as an oscillating electromagnetic field which distorted space as it traveled through the universe in the form of waves. The idea of distortions of space clearly wasn't possible within the Newtonian framework, because to fit with that theory a wave needed a medium through which to mechanically travel. To solve the problem, Maxwell and Faraday hypothesized a universal "ether" which could serve that function.[3]

In what was later proved to be a series of brilliant insights, Einstein advanced a theory that there was no ether and that light did, in fact, travel through the universe without a medium by distorting space. Einstein further postulated that this effect explained the force of gravity as well, maintaining that gravity was not a force at all in the conventional way Newton pictured it. Instead, it was the result of the way the mass of a star or planet also distorted space.

Einstein held that the moon, for example, doesn't orbit our planet because it is attracted by the earth's greater mass, which pulls it around as if it were a ball whirled on a string. Instead, the earth distorts its surrounding space, in a way that curves this space, so that the moon in reality goes in a straight line, following the laws of inertia, but still circles our planet in an orbit.

This means that we do not live in a universe in which space expands outward in all directions into infinity. The overall universe is curved by the entirety of the matter within it in an incredibly mysterious way. This means if we were to travel in a perfectly straight line in one direction long enough, over a great enough distance, we would return to the exact same place where we began. Thus space and the universe are unending, yet finite, limited, like a capsule—which begs the question: What lies outside this universe? Other universes? Other dimensional realities?

Einstein went on to establish that objective time is also warped by the influence of large bodies and by speed. The larger the gravitational field in which a clock is placed, and the faster the clock itself travels, the slower the flow of time, relative to another clock. In a now famous thought experiment, Einstein illustrated how a clock in a spaceship traveling at speeds approaching the speed of light would operate more slowly relative to a clock on earth. The occupants of the craft would notice no difference but would actually age much less during their flight than their counterparts back home.[4]

Einstein also demonstrated the constancy of the speed of light, regardless of any additional motion added or subtracted to this speed. For instance, when we are traveling in a car and throw a ball forward, the speed of the ball is the speed of the car plus the velocity of the ball after being thrust forward. Not so with light. The speed of visible light as well as all other electromagnetic phenomena is 186,000 miles per second, even if we happen to be going, say, 180,000 miles per second and shine a flashlight forward. The speed of the light coming out of the flashlight would not be the sum of its speed plus our own speed but would remain constant at 186,000 miles per second. This discovery alone, once fully grasped, shatters the old idea of a mechanical universe.

In perhaps his most revolutionary idea, Einstein also asserted that the mass of a physical object and the energy it contained were in fact interchangeable along the formula $E = mc^2$. In essence, Einstein showed that matter was nothing more than a form of light.[5]

Einstein's work was like the opening of Pandora's box. The paradigm shifted away from the concept of a mechanistic universe, and a stream of new discoveries began to prove just how mysterious the universe is.

The first new data were produced in quantum physics by such pioneers as Niels Bohr, Wolfgang Pauli, and Werner Heisenberg. Since ancient Greece, physics had ventured on a search for the basic material building blocks of nature, dividing matter into ever smaller units. The idea of the atom was confirmed, but as physicists divided the atom into the smaller particles of protons and electrons, they began to realize the surprising scale involved. As Capra relates, if the nucleus of an atom is visualized to be the size of a grain of salt, then to accurately portray the scale of a real atom, the electrons would have to be hundreds of feet away.

Just as shocking was the discovery of how these elementary particles behaved when observed. Like light itself, they seemed to act both as waves and as objects with mass, depending on the type of observation the scientists chose. In fact, early in this century, many noted quantum physicists—Heisenberg among them—began to believe that the act of observation and the intention of the scientists directly affected the behavior and existence of these elementary particles.[6]

Gradually, physicists began to question whether it made any sense to even call these entities particles at all. Certainly, they behaved like nothing that could, in any sense, be called material. For instance, if they were split apart, the separate units turned out to be twin particles of the same size and kind. Perhaps most astonishing of all is that these elementary substances have a way of communicating with themselves over time and space that is impossible according to the old mechanistic paradigm. Experiments have shown that if one particle is split in two, and one of the twins is made to change its condition, or spin, then the other automatically spins as well, even if it is very far away.[7]

In response to this discovery, physicist John Bell constructed his now famous law, known as Bell's theorem, which stipulates that once connected, atomic entities are always connected—a quite magical occurrence from the old Newtonian point of view. What's more, the latest superstring and hyperspace theories in physics bring additional mystery into this picture. They see a universe that includes multidimensions, although incredibly small, and reduce both matter and energy to pure string-like vibrations.[8]

As one might expect, this new description of the universe by the physicists has begun to affect the other disciplines as well, particularly biology. As part of the old paradigm, biology had reduced life to the mechanics of chemical reactions. And Darwin's mechanistic theory of evolution had allowed biology to explain the existence of the wide range of life-forms on this planet, including human beings, in terms of random processes in nature, without reference to the spiritual.

That life in some way evolved from smaller to larger forms on this planet is irrefutable—the fossil record is clear. But the description of the new, mysterious universe by physicists has brought into question Darwin's secular formulation of how evolution worked.

In Darwin's conception, mutations randomly occurred in the offspring of the members of all species, giving these descendants slightly different traits. If the traits proved to be advantageous, those individuals survived at a greater rate, and ultimately the new trait became established as a general characteristic of the species. According to Darwin, for instance, a few of the ancestors of the modern-day giraffe randomly grew long necks, and because this development proved to be an advantage (reaching more plentiful sources of food), the offspring of these animals survived at a greater rate and eventually all species of that kind had long necks.

In the secular, nonmysterious universe, evolution could be conceived of in no other way. But now, various problems can be seen with these ideas. One difficulty is that recent data projections show that a completely random process would have been very slow, and it would have taken life-forms much longer to reach the stage they have than the amount of time life has been evolving on earth. Another problem is that the fossil record does not show the missing links or transitional creatures that should be there to reflect a gradual change of a species from one form to another.[9]

Certainly, multicelled organisms followed single-celled organisms, and reptiles and mammals didn't emerge until after fish and amphibians developed. But the process seemed to jump from one fully formed species to the next, with the new species appearing at the same time in many different places in the world. The mysterious aspects of the universe described by the new physics suggest that perhaps evolution is proceeding more purposefully than Darwin had supposed.

Besides biology, the new physics began to affect many other disciplines as well—especially psychology and sociology—because it so dramatically changed our conception of the outer universe in which we live. No longer can we think of ourselves as living in a simple world of solid, material stuff. If we are awake, we know that everything around us is a mysterious vibrating pattern of energy, the stuff of light . . . and that includes us.

UNIVERSAL ENERGY, *CH'I*, AND THE HUMAN ENERGY FIELD

There are direct parallels between the views of the new physics and the description of reality offered by the Eastern philosophies of Hinduism, Buddhism, and Taoism. The new physics describes the world of matter and form in terms of a quantum field of energy comprising everything. Below the surface of the things of the world, there are no basic building blocks of nature; there is only an interconnecting web of energy relationships.

The major religious philosophies of the East hold essentially the same view, but instead of coming to this conclusion as a result of objective experimentation, they reached it after centuries of careful inner observation.

Eastern thought proclaims that the universe on which we gaze is essentially one indivisible whole, consisting of one life or spiritual force—because that is what it can be experienced to be.

Each of these religions has its own method of attaining a greater connection with the larger universe. But all assert that human beings, while being intimately connected to this subtle energy, called *prana* or *ch'i* (or *ki*), are usually cut off from its higher levels. Various disciplines of these Eastern religions—meditation and martial arts, for instance—are designed to awaken this relationship, and spectacular results have been documented. Certain Eastern Yogis have displayed unbelievable feats of strength, control over their bodies, and the ability to withstand extreme heat or cold.[10]

Some Eastern systems assert that the energy circulating through human beings can actually be observed in the form of an encircling field of light or aura. This energy is often perceived as colored light emanating from each human being, and the distinctive shape or tone of this light reflects the nature of the individual's inner being and character.

By the 1950s, as the descriptions of the new physics began to circulate in the mass media, suddenly these esoteric assertions of the East, based strictly on inner observation, began to be taken more seriously by psychologists and sociologists in the West. The East had created a system in which the potential of the human being was much more open-ended and far-reaching, and as these concepts became known, the old paradigm began to splinter further in the other disciplines. The new physics had given us a new conception of the surrounding universe, and now a similar movement in the human sciences was about to bring us a new understanding of ourselves.

THE HUMAN POTENTIAL MOVEMENT

At the midpoint of the twentieth century, the predominant focus of psychology in the West was on the study of the human mind in relation to our actions in the outer world—in other words, the investigation of our behavior. Following the mechanistic paradigm, psychologists were looking for a key principle or formula to which all human action in the world could be reduced, which had earlier led to the stimulus/response model of behaviorism.

The only other major approach to the study of human psychology was being conducted in psychiatry, following the medical pathology model first created by Sigmund Freud. A late-nineteenth-century thinker, Freud had looked deeply into the structure of the mind itself, basing his theories on reductionistic and biological concepts acceptable to the mechanistic paradigm.

Freud was the first to postulate that the traumas of

childhood often resulted in neurotic fears and reactions of which human beings were generally unaware. He concluded that mankind's behavior was motivated simply by the drive to increase pleasure and to avoid pain.

During the late 1950s, however, the mysteries revealed by the new physics, the growing influence of the Eastern philosophies, and the dual movements of existentialism and phenomenology in Western philosophy inspired a third theoretical development in psychology. This new orientation was led by Abraham Maslow, who, with a host of other thinkers and writers, argued for a more complete way of studying human consciousness.[11]

Rejecting behaviorism as too abstract, and Freud's theories as too obsessed with sublimated sexual desires, these scientists wanted to study the mind with the focus on perception itself. Here they were deeply influenced by the East, where consciousness was studied from the inside, the way every human being actually experiences his or her own consciousness. As we live our lives, we look out on the world through our senses, interpret what is happening around us based on our memories and expectations, and use our thoughts and intuitions to act. This new psychological approach was called humanism, and it grew by leaps and bounds through the 1960s and 1970s.

The humanists didn't deny that we are often unconscious of what motivates our behavior. They agreed that human beings tend to restrict their own experience, often repeating scripts and reaction patterns designed to reduce anxiety. But the humanists also focused on how humans might liberate their outlooks and transcend their scripts and open up to the higher human experience that was available.

This new perspective led to a rediscovery of the work of Carl Jung, the Swiss psychoanalyst, who broke with Freud in 1912 to develop his own theories, including the principle of synchronicity. According to Jung, as we look out on the world, our inner urges are not just to avoid pain and maximize hedonistic pleasure, as Freud thought, although at the lowest levels of consciousness it may look that way. Our greatest urge, Jung asserted, is toward psychological wholeness and self-actualization of our inner potential.

In this journey, we are aided by already established pathways in the brain, which he called *archetypes*. As we grow psychologically, we can realize, or activate, these archetypes and in so doing progress toward self-actualization. The first stage of growth is one of differentiation, during which we become aware of ourselves in the cultural milieu in which we are born and begin to individuate. This means we have to find a niche for ourselves in the world we learned in childhood, a process that includes becoming educated, assessing the economy, and finding a way to make a living.

As we do this, we sharpen our ego power and our will, replacing our learned set of automatic reactions with a logical way of interpreting events that becomes our own way of standing out, extending our self in the world as a unique person with unique views. This stage is at first somewhat narcissistic (selfish) and often in-flated (egotistical) but eventually fully activates what Jung called the Hero archetype. At that point, we are ready to find something important to do in the culture; we feel proud and determined about accomplishing it.

As we continue to grow, we progress beyond the Hero phase and activate what Jung called the Self arche-type, a developmental step during which we move past a self-concept based on mastering our milieu. Instead, we enter a more inwardly directed consciousness where intuition and logic become partners, and our goals be-come more in line with our inner images and dreams of what we really want to do.

This is the phase he described as self-actualization, and it was here that he spoke about the higher percep-tion of synchronicity. Although glimpsed at every level, the perception of meaningful coincidences becomes most instructive during this phase. At this stage, the events of our lives begin to respond to our readiness for growth, and the synchronicity begins to occur more frequently.[12]

Reinforced by Jung, the full picture of how humans get stuck during this process began to emerge. Follow-ing the line of discovery from Freud and Otto Rank through Norman O. Brown and Ernest Becker, we could see what happens. Humans create particular lifestyle beliefs and behaviors (scripts) that they inflexibly hold on to as their way of pushing anxiety out of consciousness. These range from uncontrollable fetishes and neurotic habits to more normal, fixed religious ideas and philosophical beliefs. What these scripts have in common is their intractable nature and their resistance to rational debate or discussion.

The humanists further discovered that human society is characterized by irrational power struggles designed solely to keep these scripts intact. Here a wave of thinkers, including Gregory Bateson and R. D. Laing, began to map out this process.[13]

One key discovery was called the *double-bind effect*, during which humans discount every idea offered by others in order to dominate the interaction. As Laing demonstrated, when this habit is perpetrated by parents on their children, tragic effects often occur. When every possible action a child offers is criticized, the child retreats into extreme defensiveness and develops excessive reaction patterns created to fight back. When these children grow up, their defensiveness and need to control every situation lead them to unconsciously use double-bind techniques themselves, especially toward their own children, and thus the condition perpetuates itself across many generations.

These interaction psychologists found that this mode of human communication was epidemic in human society, creating a culture where everyone was defensively trying to control and dominate everyone else. In these conditions, self-actualization and higher creativity were limited, because most people spent their time struggling to dominate others and reinforce their scripts, instead of opening up to the greater possibilities available in experience and in relationships among people.

Over several decades, these findings were extensively popularized, especially in the United States. Dr. Eric Berne's book *Games People Play* surveyed the most common scripts and manipulations and described them in great detail. Thomas Harris's *I'm OK/You're OK* explained how transactional analysis could be used to analyze the true nature of human conversations and move toward a more mature way of interacting.[14] A new awareness of the quality of our interactions began to make its way through the culture, advancing the idea that all of us can transcend these habits.

As the humanistic idea that we can find a higher level of experience blossomed, the mystery of our existence itself became a subject of wide discussion among the humanists. It was at this point that Darwin's formulation of evolution was reevaluated, thrown into question by thinkers such as Pierre Teilhard de Chardin and Sri Aurobindo, both of whom maintained that evolution was not arbitrary but was moving in a purposeful direction. These thinkers have argued that the course of life from the early organisms into more complex animals and plants had purpose, that human beings were not accidents of nature, and that our social evolution, including our journey into the higher realms of spiritual experience, was an outcome for which all of evolution had been aiming.[15]

One current theorist who has offered an understanding of life that supports this thesis is Rupert Sheldrake. According to Sheldrake's theory of life, biological forms are created and sustained through morphogenic fields. These fields are nonlocal in nature and create an invisible structure which molecules and cells and organs follow as they differentiate and specialize to create a particular life-form. What's more, this field evolves over time as each generation of a species not only is structured by this underlying field but amends this field as it overcomes challenges in the environment.

For example, a fish, in order to thrive in its biological niche, might need to evolve new fins in order to swim faster. In Sheldrake's system, the will of the fish would initiate a change in the morphogenic field of that species that would be reflected in her progeny growing those exact fins. This theory introduces the possibility that the leaps evident in the fossil record might have also occurred in this way—as members of a given species create a morphogenic field that produces not just additional traits but a jump into a different life-form altogether. For example, some particular fish might have reached the limit of their evolution in water and produced progeny that were actually a new species: amphibians, who could crawl onto the land.

According to Sheldrake, this progress could account for social evolution in humans as well. Throughout history, we humans, like other life-forms, have pushed the outer envelope of our knowledge, always striving to evolve toward a fuller understanding of our environment and the actualization of our own inner potential. At any one time, the level of human ability and awareness can be thought of as being defined by the shared morphogenic field. As individuals actualize particular abilities—running faster, picking up on others' thoughts, receiving intuitions—the morphogenic field is shifted forward not just for them but for all other humans. That's why inventions and discoveries are often put forward at the same time in history by individuals who have no contact with each other.

Here the findings of modern physics and the latest research by scientists on the effects of prayer and intention begin to merge. We are intimately connected with the universe and with each other, and our influence on our world with our thoughts is more powerful than anyone ever dreamed.

THE RESPONSIVE UNIVERSE

In the last several decades, researchers in psychology have begun to seriously study the effect of our intentions on the physical universe. Some of the first findings in this regard occurred in the area of biofeedback. Through hundreds of studies, it has been shown that we can influence many of our bodily functions formerly thought to be totally controlled by the autonomic nervous system, including heart rate, blood pressure, immune system, and brain waves. Almost any process we can monitor showed some susceptibility to our will.[16]

Recent research, however, has shown that our connectedness and influence go much further than that. Our intentions can also affect other people's bodies, their minds, and the shape of events in the world. The new physics has shown that we are connected in a way that transcends the limits of space and time. Bell's theorem seems to apply just as well to our thoughts as to the operation of elementary particles.

No one has contributed more to the popularization of this new understanding than Dr. Larry Dossey, who has written a series of books focusing on our powers of intention and prayer. By surveying past and present research from F. W. H. Myers to Lawrence LeShan, from J. B. Rhine to the Princeton Engineering Anomalies Research Laboratory, Dossey has presented a provocative summary of evidence that we can reach across space, and sometimes time, to affect the world.[17]

In one particular study cited in his book *Recovering the Soul,* Dossey describes a group of subjects who were assembled to test their ability to receive information over great distances. Asked to name a card that was randomly drawn by a subject in another location, other subjects, hundreds of miles away, were not only able to discern the card at rates greater than chance, but often received the information even before the card was actually drawn.

In other studies designed to test this ability further, subjects were able to discern a group of numbers produced by a random-number generator even before the numbers were produced. The implications of this and similar studies are of extreme significance, because they provide evidence for abilities many of us have repeatedly experienced. Not only are we connected to each other telepathically, but we also have a precognitive ability; we seem to be able to pick up images or hunches about upcoming events, especially if they affect our own lives and growth.[18]

Yet our abilities are even more far-reaching. We can not only receive information about the world with our minds, we can mentally affect the world as well. Dossey cites one particular study, now quite well known, that was carried out by Dr. Randolph Byrd at San Francisco General Hospital. In this study, one group of heart patients was prayed for by a team of volunteers, and a control group of patients received no prayer.[19] Dossey reports that the prayed-for group was five times less likely to need antibiotics and three times less likely to develop fluid in the lungs than the control group. In addition, none of the prayed-for group needed to be artificially ventilated, while twelve members of the control group did.

Other studies cited by Dossey showed that the power of prayer and intention works equally well with plants (increasing the number of seeds that sprout); bacteria (increasing growth rates); and inanimate objects (affecting the random patterns Styrofoam balls make when they fall).[20]

One group of studies showed something else that is especially interesting. Though our ability to affect the world works in both cases, nondirective intention (that is, holding the idea that the *very best* should happen without injecting our opinion) works better than directive intention (holding the idea that a specific outcome should occur). This seems to indicate that there is a principle or law built into our connectedness with the rest of the universe that keeps our egos in check.

The studies Dossey cites also suggest that we must have some personal knowledge of the subject of our prayer and that overall intention that flows from a sense of connectedness with the divine, or with one's higher self, seems to work best. In addition, experiments seem to confirm that our intentions have a cumulative effect. In other words, subjects who are prayed for longer benefit more than those who are prayed for less.

Most important, Dossey cites studies indicating that our general assumptions act on the world just like our more conscious intentions or prayers. The famous Oak School experiment is a case in point. In this study, teachers were told that a certain group of pupils, identified by testing, would be able to make the greatest progress during the school year. In truth, the teachers were given a list of pupils chosen completely at random. At the end of the year, these students in fact showed significant increases not only in their performance (which might be explained by the teachers having given them extra attention) but in IQ scores designed to test purely innate ability as well.[21] In other words, the teacher's assumptions about their students shifted their actual potential to learn.

Unfortunately, this effect seems to operate in a negative direction as well. In his recent book *Be Careful What You Pray For, You Just Might Get It,* Dossey points out studies that show that our unconscious assumptions can harm others. One important example is when we pray for someone to change his mind or to stop what he is doing before we carefully investigate whether he might be correct on the issue. These thoughts go out and create self-doubt in the other person. The same thing happens when we have negative thoughts about how another person looks or acts. Often these are opinions we would never express to anyone directly, but because we are all connected, these thoughts go out like daggers to influence a person's concepts about himself, and possibly even his actual behavior.[22]

This means, of course, that we can also negatively influence the reality of our own situations with our unconscious thoughts. When we think negatively about our personal abilities, our looks, or our prospects in the future, these thoughts influence how we feel and what happens to us in a very real way.

LIVING THE NEW REALITY

Here, then, we can see the larger picture being offered by the new science. Now when we linger outside in our yards or stroll through a park admiring the landscape on a bright sunny day, we must see a new world. No longer can we think of the universe we live in as expanding outward in all directions to infinity. We know that the universe is physically unending but curved in a way that makes it limited and finite. We live inside a bubble of space/time, and like the hyperspace physicist, we intuit other dimensions. And when we look around at the forms within this universe, we can no longer see solid matter but energy stuff. Everything, including ourselves, is nothing more than a field of energy, of light, all interacting and influencing each other.

Actually, most of these descriptions of the new reality have already been confirmed by our own experience. We all have moments, for instance, when we can perceive that others have picked up on our thoughts, or times when we know what others feel or are about to say. Similarly, we have times when we know something is about to happen or potentially could happen, and these precognitions are often followed by hunches telling us where we should go or what we should do to be in exactly the right place at the right time. Most significant, we know that our attitude and intention about others is extremely important. As we shall see later, when we think positively, uplifting ourselves and others in the process, incredible events begin to unfold.

Our challenge is to put all of this into daily practice, to integrate it into how we live our lives every day. We live in an intelligent, responsive, energy-dynamic universe, in which other people's expectations and assumptions radiate outward to influence us.

The next step, therefore, in our journey toward living the new spiritual awareness is to see the human world of energy and expectation and drama for what it is, and to learn to negotiate this world in a more effective way.

5

OVERCOMING THE POWER STRUGGLE

The great achievement of the interaction psychologists was to identify and explain the way humans tend to compete and dominate each other because of a deep existential insecurity. It has been from the East, however, that we have gained further clarification of the psychology underlying this phenomenon.

As both science and mysticism demonstrate, humans are in essence a field of energy. Yet the East maintains that our normal energy levels are weak and flat until we open up to the absolute energies available in the universe. When this opening occurs, our *ch'i*—or perhaps we should call it our level of quantum energy—is raised to a height that resolves our existential insecurity. But until then we move around seeking additional energy from other people.

Let's begin our discussion by looking at what really happens when two humans interact. There is an old mystical saying that where attention goes, energy flows. Thus, when two people turn their attention to one another, they literally merge energy fields, pooling their energy. The issue quickly becomes: Who is going to control this accumulated energy? If one can dominate, managing to get the other to defer to his point of view, to look at the world in his way, through his eyes, then this individual has captured both energies as his own. He feels an immediate rush of power, security, self-worth, even euphoria.

But those positive feelings are won at the other person's expense, for the dominated individual feels off center, anxious, and drained of energy.[1] All of us have felt this way at one time or another. When we are forced to defer to someone who has manipulated us into confusion, thrown us off balance, shown us up, we suddenly feel deflated. And our natural tendency is to try to win energy back from the dominator, usually by any means necessary.

This process of psychological domination can be observed everywhere, and it is the underlying source of all irrational conflict in the human world, from the level of individuals and families all the way to cultures and nations. If we look realistically at society, therefore, we see it is an energy-competitive world, with people manipulating other people in very ingenious (and usually quite unconscious) ways. In light of the new understanding of the universe, we can also see that most of the manipulations used in this regard, most of the *games people play,* are the result of basic life assumptions. In other words, they form the individual's field of intention.

When we move into interaction with another human being, we must keep all this in mind. Every person is an energy field consisting of a set of assumptions and beliefs that radiate outward and influence the world. This includes beliefs about what an individual thinks other people are like, and how to win in conversation.

Everyone has a unique set of assumptions and style of interaction in this regard, which I have called *control dramas.* I believe that these "dramas" fall along a continuum ranging from very passive to very aggressive.

THE POOR ME

The most passive of the control dramas is the victim strategy, or what I have called the Poor Me. In this drama, rather than competing for energy directly, the person seeks to win deference and attention through the manipulation of sympathy.

We can always tell when we enter the energy field of a Poor Me because we are immediately drawn into a particular kind of dialogue in which we are pulled off center. Out of the blue, we begin to feel guilty for no reason, as though we are being cast into that role by the other person. The individual might say, "Well, I expected you to call yesterday, but you never did," or "I had all these bad things happen to me and you were nowhere to be found." He might even add, "All these other bad things are about to happen to me, and you probably won't be around then, either."

Depending on the kind of relationship we have with the person, the phrases might be shaped around a wide range of subject matter. If the person is a work associate, the content may refer to his or her being overwhelmed with work production or meeting deadlines—a situation with which you are not helping. If the person is a casual acquaintance, he or she may just pull you into a conversation about how rotten life is going in general. Dozens of variations exist, but the basic tone and strategy are the same. Always it is some kind of bid for sympathy and an assertion that you are somehow responsible.

The obvious strategy in the Poor Me drama is to throw us off balance and win our energy by creating a feeling of guilt or doubt on our part. By buying into that guilt, we are stopping and looking through the other person's eyes at his or her world. As soon as we do this, the person gets to feel the boost of our energy added to his or her own and so feels more secure.

Remember that this drama is almost completely unconscious. It flows from a personal view of the world and a strategy for controlling others adopted in early childhood. To the Poor Me, the world is a place where people can't be counted on to meet one's needs for nurturing and well-being, and it is too scary a place to risk pursuing these needs directly or assertively. In the Poor Me's world, the only reasonable way of acting is to bid for sympathy through guilt trips and perceived slights.

Unfortunately, because of the effect on the world of these unconscious beliefs and intentions, very often the same kind of abusive people the Poor Me fears are exactly the ones that they allow into their lives. And the events that befall them are often traumatic. The universe responds by producing exactly the kind of world the person expects, and in this way, the drama is always circular and self-validating. The Poor Me is caught unknowingly in a vicious trap.

Dealing with the Poor Me

In dealing with the Poor Me, it is important to remind ourselves that the purpose of the drama is to win energy. We must begin with the willingness to consciously give the Poor Me energy as we talk with him; this is the fastest way to break the drama. (Sending energy is a precise process that we will discuss in Chapter 9.)

The next thing we must do is to consider whether the guilt trip is justified. Certainly, there will be plenty of cases in our lives when we should feel concern over having let someone down or sympathy for someone in a difficult situation. But these realities must be determined by us, not by someone else. Only we can decide to what extent and when we are responsible to help someone in need.

Once we have given the Poor Me energy and determined that we are facing a control drama in action, the next step is to name the game—that is, to make the control drama itself the topic of conversation.[2] No unconscious game can be sustained if it is pulled into consciousness and placed on the table for discussion. This can be done with a statement such as, "You know, right now I feel as though you think I should feel guilty."

Here we must be prepared to proceed with courage, because while we are seeking to deal honestly with the situation, the other person might interpret what we say as a rejection. In this case, the typical reaction might be "Oh, well, I knew you really didn't like me." In other cases, the person may feel insulted and angry.

It is very important, in my opinion, to appeal to the person to listen and to continue the conversation. But this can only work if we are constantly giving this person the energy he wants during the conversation. Above all, we must persevere if we want the quality of the relationship to improve. In the best case, the person will hear what we are saying as we point out the drama and be able to open up to a higher state of self-awareness.

THE ALOOF

A slightly less passive control drama is the Aloof's. We know we have entered the energy field of someone using this strategy when we begin a conversation and realize we can't really get a straight answer. The person we are talking to is distant, detached, cryptic in her responses. If we ask about her personal background, for instance, we get a very vague summary, such as "I traveled around a bit," with no further elaboration.

As we have this conversation, we sense that we have to ask a follow-up question, even for the simplest of inquiries. Maybe we have to say, "Well, where have you traveled?" And we receive the reply, "Many places."

Here we can clearly see the strategy of the Aloof. The person constantly creates a vague and mysterious aura around herself, forcing us to pour energy into digging to get information normally shared in a casual manner. When we do this, we are intensely focusing on the person's world, looking through her eyes, hoping to understand her background, and so we are giving her the boost of energy that she desires.

We must remember, however, that not everyone who is being vague or who refuses to give us information about herself is using an Aloof drama. She may just want to remain anonymous for some other reason. Every person has the right to privacy and to share with others only as much as she wants.

Using this distancing strategy to gain energy, however, is something altogether different. For the Aloof, it is a method of manipulation that seeks to lure us in, yet keep us at a distance. If we conclude that a person just doesn't want to talk with us, for instance—and so we shift our attention elsewhere—very often the Aloof will come back into interaction with us, saying something designed to draw us back into the interaction so the energy can keep flowing her way.

As with the Poor Me, the Aloof strategy comes from situations in the past. Usually, the Aloof could not share freely as a child because it was threatening or dangerous to do so. In that kind of environment, the Aloof learned to be constantly vague in communication with others while at the same time finding a way to be listened to in order to win energy from others.

As with the Poor Me, the Aloof strategy is a set of unconscious assumptions about the world. The Aloof believes that the world is full of people who can't be trusted with intimate information. She thinks the information will be used against her at a later date, or will be the basis of criticism. And as always, these assumptions flow out from the Aloof to influence the kinds of events that occur, fulfilling the unconscious intention.

Dealing with the Aloof

To deal effectively with someone using an Aloof drama, we must again remember to begin by sending energy. By sending loving energy rather than becoming defensive ourselves, we relieve the pressure to continue the manipulation. With the pressure off, we can begin again, naming the game and bringing the drama into awareness by making it the topic of conversation.

As before, we can expect one of two reactions. First, the Aloof may flee the interaction and sever all communication. This, of course, is always a risk that must be taken, because to say anything else is to continue to play the game. In this case, we can only hope that our directness will begin a new pattern that will lead to self-awareness.

The Aloof's other reaction may be to stay in communication but to deny being aloof. In this case, as always, we must consider the truth of what the person is saying. However, if we are sure of our perception, we must hold fast and continue to dialogue with the person. Out of the conversation, we hope, a new pattern will be established.

THE INTERROGATOR

A more aggressive control drama, one that is pervasive in modern society, is that of the Interrogator. In this manipulation strategy, one uses criticism to gain energy from others.

In the presence of an Interrogator, we always get a distinct feeling that we are being monitored. Simultaneously, we may feel as though we are being cast in the role of someone who is inadequate, or unable to handle our own lives.

We feel this way because the person we are interacting with has pulled us into a reality where he feels that most people are making huge mistakes with their lives and he must correct the situation. For instance, the Interrogator may say, "You know, you really don't dress well enough for the kind of job you have," or "I've noticed you don't really keep your house very neat." Just as easily, the criticism could involve how we do our jobs, the way we talk, or a wide range of personal characteristics. It doesn't really matter. Anything will work as long as the criticism throws us off balance and makes us unsure of ourselves.

The unconscious strategy of the Interrogator is to point out something about us that gives us pause, hoping that we will buy into the criticism and adopt the Interrogator's view of the world. When this happens, we begin to look at the situation through the eyes of the Interrogator and thus give him energy. The Interrogator's aim is to become the dominant judge of other people's lives so that as soon as interaction begins, others immediately defer to his worldview, providing a steady flow of energy.

Like the other dramas, this one springs from projected assumptions about the world. This person believes that the world is not safe or orderly unless he is watching everyone's behavior and attitude, and making corrections. In this world, he is the hero, the only one paying attention and making sure things are done carefully and with perfection. Usually, the Interrogator comes from a family in which his parental figures were absent or not attentive to his needs. In this insecure void of energy, the Interrogator gained attention and energy in the only way possible: by pointing out errors and criticizing the family's behavior.

When the child is grown, he carries with him these assumptions about how the world is and what people are like, and these assumptions in turn create that kind of reality in the Interrogator's life.

Dealing with the Interrogator

Handling the Interrogator is a matter of staying centered enough to tell him how we are feeling in his presence. Again, the key is to keep from assuming a defensive posture ourselves and to send loving energy as we explain that we feel monitored and criticized by him.

The Interrogator, too, may have several different reactions. First, he may deny being critical at all, even in the face of examples. Again, we must consider the possibility that we are wrong and somehow hearing putdowns when none are intended. If, on the other hand, we are sure of our perspective, then we can only explain our position, hoping that a genuine dialogue can begin.

Another reaction the Interrogator might have is to turn the tables and call us critical. If this happens, we must again consider whether the accusation is true. However, if, as before, we see this is not happening, then we must return to our discussion of how the other person makes us feel in his presence.

A third reaction that the Interrogator might have is to argue that the criticisms are valid and need to be given and that we are avoiding facing up to our own faults. Again, we have to consider the truth of this statement, but if we are sure of our position, several examples can be given to show that the Interrogator's criticisms have been either unnecessary or inappropriately given.

Each of us will face situations in which we sense that others are doing something that appears not in their best interest. We might feel that we should intervene to point out the error. The key factor here is how we intervene. We are learning, I believe, to make very unassuming statements, such as, "If my tires were bald like this, I would buy a new set," or "When I was in a situation like yours, I quit my job before finding another and later regretted it."

There are ways to intervene that do not take the person out of his centered viewpoint or undermine his confidence, the way the Interrogator does, and this difference must be explained to the Interrogator. Again, this person may sever the relationship rather than hear what we are saying, but this is a risk we have to take in order to stay true to our own experience.

THE INTIMIDATOR

The most aggressive control drama is the Intimidator's strategy. We can tell when we enter the energy field of such a person because we not only feel drained or uncomfortable; we feel unsafe, perhaps even in danger. The world turns ominous, threatening, out of control. The Intimidator will say and do things that suggest she might erupt in rage or violence at any moment. She may tell stories of harming others or show us the extent of her anger by breaking furniture or throwing items across the room.

The strategy of the Intimidator is to win our attention and thus our energy by creating an environment in which we feel so threatened we are totally focused on her. When someone gives off the impression that she might go out of control or do something dangerous at any minute, most of us watch this person very carefully. If we are in a conversation with such a person, we usually defer to her perspective very quickly. Of course, when we look through her eyes, trying to discern what she might do (in order to keep ourselves safe), she receives the boost of energy that she most desperately needs.

This strategy of intimidation is usually developed in a past environment of severe energy deprivation, most commonly involving relationships with other Intimidators who are dominating and abusive, and where no other strategy works to win energy back. Guilt-tripping as a Poor Me doesn't work; no one cares. Certainly, no one notices if you are playing Aloof. And any attempt at Interrogating is met with anger and hostility. The only solution is to endure the lack of energy until one is big enough to intimidate in one's own right.

The world the Intimidator sees is one of random violence and hostility. It is a world in which one is lost in supreme isolation, where everyone rejects and no one cares—which is exactly what these assumptions bring into the Intimidator's life, over and over.

Dealing with the Intimidator

Confronting the Intimidator is a special case. Because of the obvious danger, in most cases it is better simply to remove oneself from the presence of an Intimidator. If one is in a long-term relationship with an Intimidator, the best course is usually to place the situation in the hands of a professional. The therapeutic plan of action, of course, is much the same as with the other dramas. Success with such an individual usually involves making her feel safe, giving supportive energy, and bringing the reality of her drama into awareness. Unfortunately, there are many Intimidators still out there who are receiving no help, and who live in alternating states of fear and rage.

Many of these individuals wind up in the criminal justice system, and certainly it is wise to keep these people away from society. But a system that keeps them locked up with no therapeutic intervention and then lets them out again does not understand or address the root of the problem.[3]

OVERCOMING OUR
CONTROL DRAMA

Most of us, throughout life, hear various complaints from others about our behavioral patterns. The human tendency is to ignore or rationalize away these complaints in order to go on with our preferred style of life. Even now, when knowledge of self-defeating scripts and habits is becoming a greater part of human awareness, we find it very difficult to view our personal behavior in an objective manner.

In the case of severe control dramas in which a person has sought professional help, crisis reactions can undo years of progress and growth in counseling as the old patterns, once thought conquered, reappear. In fact, one of the emerging revelations among professional counselors is that true progress takes more than the catharsis that occurs during the personal exploration of early childhood traumas.[4] We now know that to end these unconscious attempts to gain energy and security, we must focus on the deeper, existential basis of the problem and look beyond intellectual insight to tap a new source of security that can function regardless of external circumstances.

Here I am referring to a different type of catharsis— one that the mystics have pointed to throughout history and one that we are rapidly hearing more about. Knowing what we do about the energy competitions in human society, our challenge is to look closely at ourselves, to identify our particular set of assumptions and the intentions that constitute our drama, and to find another experience that allows us to open up to our energy within.

6

EXPERIENCING THE MYSTICAL

The idea of the mystical experience began its journey into the mass consciousness of Western culture in the late 1950s, chiefly as a result of the popularization of Hindu, Buddhist, and Taoist traditions by such writers and thinkers as Carl Jung, Alan Watts, and D. T. Suzuki.[1] This dissemination has continued in subsequent decades with a multitude of works, including those of Paramahansa Yogananda, J. Krishnamurti, and Ram Dass,[2] all affirming the existence of an inner mystical encounter that can be experienced individually.

During these same decades, a large, popular audience also became interested in the rich esoteric tradition of spirituality we have in the West as well. The thoughts of St. Francis of Assisi, Meister Eckhart, Emanuel Swedenborg, and Edmund Bucke have all gained attention because these thinkers, like the Eastern mystics, all affirm the existence of inner transformation.[3]

I believe that we have finally reached a point where the idea of a personal transcendent experience—variously called enlightenment, nirvana, satori, transcendence, and cosmic consciousness—has reached a significant level of acceptance; it has become an integral part of our new spiritual awareness. We have, as a culture, begun to accept mystical encounters as something real and available to all human beings.

MOVING FROM IDEA TO EXPERIENCE

As a culture, we in the West began our exploration of mystical experience with long intellectual discussions and speculations. We needed to familiarize ourselves with new concepts and were struggling to find a personal way to integrate such notions with our Western idea of what was real. These conversations stimulated our interest and threw new light on our own abstract spiritual ideas, such concepts as *communion with God, seeking the kingdom within,* and *being born again.*

In a sense, however, these discussions remained in the left-brained realm of abstract acceptance.[4] Even though many of us intuited the possibility of such encounters, only a few actually experienced real moments of transcendence. Yet the popularizations continued, and we have been moving, in my opinion, ever closer to a popular actualization of this experience. We now hear precise personal descriptions of mystical encounters not just from books or lecturers, but from those we know. Because of this, the idea is becoming more of a lived reality—affirmed in others and expressed with a consistency that tells us that the inner, transcendent experience is something that really happens to real people.

This is helping us reach a new level of honesty, especially with ourselves. If we look within and realize that we haven't yet had such an encounter, then our search for the transcendent experience can become a top priority. And I think we also realize that the inner, transformative encounter can occur in many ways, along many paths.

What is important is not the particular religion, practice, or activity that leads us there, but the heightened, mystical perception that is the destination. It is the experience itself that expands our awareness and imbues us with a sense of security, well-being, and clarity undreamed of before it occurs.

EXPERIENCING TRANSCENDENCE IN SPORTS

Everyone's talking about the "zone" experience that can be achieved in the course of sports and recreational activities. During this experience, we find ourselves shifting in awareness, usually beginning with a feeling of total immersion in the action. Our bodies begin to feel different, as though they are moving more efficiently, more gracefully, more completely in unison with our goal.

Rather than being a separate part of the activity, watching the action and reacting accordingly, we begin to feel a part of the flow, part of the whole moment, as if we know in advance what is going to happen, where the ball is going, what the other players are going to do. In this way, we react spontaneously, in concert, so as to be in just the right place at the right time.

Often, time itself begins to change, slowing down. In ordinary states, we usually have the sense that the game is going too fast, that we are constantly hurrying to catch up, struggling to think ahead. But in the zone—or during a peak experience—we have the sense that time slows down as our consciousness rises to a higher, more omnipotent point of view. In this state, we seem to have all the time in the world to hit the ball or jump for the rebound. When we observe athletes who are playing at this level, we sense that they defy gravity, hang in the air longer than seems possible, and make spectacular moves that get them to a new position instantly.

In the last two decades, a host of books has emerged describing the inner aspect of every sport, and this is especially true of golf. Michael Murphy's *Golf in the Kingdom* has sold over a million copies because it so perfectly describes the inner experience associated with this sport.[5] I believe that golf's growing popularity around the world is because of the game's special challenges and rewards. Somehow we have to learn to hit a little white ball, only an inch in diameter, with a lengthy club, whose head is not much larger than the ball itself. Advocates often insist that golf is the most difficult of all games, precisely for that reason. Granted, in golf we attempt to hit a ball that is not moving, but this in itself creates additional difficulty: we are alone with ourselves, facing the pressure of the long swing and the relatively narrow path to a distant target. In other games, the rhythm of the action and the ball's movement can keep us loose and in a pattern of reaction. On the links, we are constantly having to fight the ill effects of fear, tightness, and thinking too much, all while having to begin the swing from a position of being perfectly still.

Perhaps it is this inner challenge that makes golf's attraction so immense and the zone experience so identifiable once we reach it. There is no mistaking the state of mind in which the body takes over and begins to work effortlessly, and we seem to be willing the ball to its target.

DANCE AND THE MOVEMENT ARTS

Everyone has seen dancers who seem to float in the air and martial artists who achieve acts of total coordination. These activities represent another pathway through which individuals report they have achieved a transcendent experience. Like the traditional whirling dervishes of the Islamic Sufi order, many forms of dance bring us out of our ordinary consciousness and connect us with a higher spiritual awareness within.

Dancers report the same sense of expanded consciousness that people experience with sports, especially a sense of supreme muscular coordination. In addition, many people report a kind of ecstatic experience during free-form dancing in which the movements are spontaneous and thought is pushed far into the background. During these moments, we seem to be the dance, expressing an inner aspect of our being that feels like a higher self.

The martial arts conceive these experiences in terms of cultivating a higher degree of spiritual energy and using it in the act of movement and feats of strength. Through repeated motion and attention, these practices gradually move us into a conscious letting-go of ordinary ways of concentration and being.

PRAYER AND MEDITATION

Prayer and meditation, two of the most traditional pathways, often lead to the experience of inner transformation. Every major religion in the world uses one of these forms of communication with the divine. Usually, when we pray, we call upon a divine creator or force for some reason; we ask help, guidance, or forgiveness in an active sense. We have something in mind that we want. But we also pray for the pure experience of communion or connection.

When it is practiced in this latter sense, prayer is very similar to meditation—it calms the mind, pushes away the chatter of the ego, reaches out for a higher connection. Some religious traditions suggest using a mantra (repeated words or sounds that we invoke or focus upon) to aid these efforts. As other thoughts emerge, the meditator is instructed to let them pass and come back to a focus on the mantra and on the quietness of meditation. At some point, random thoughts begin to cease and the meditator goes deeper into relaxation until the sense of the ordinary self begins to expand into the experience of transcendence.

Both active prayer and meditation can lead to an inner transformative experience, where our connection to the divine is perceived in an ecstatic manner of being one with the whole of the universe.

SACRED SITES

Of all the pathways to the inner mystical experience, the shift of consciousness that sometimes occurs at sacred and wilderness sites on the earth may be the most intriguing. Of course, in one sense, all places on our planet are sacred, and mystical transformation can occur anywhere. Yet throughout history, certain locations have proved especially conducive to such states of mystical awareness.

Usually, these sites have very specific physical characteristics. First, they are almost always incredibly beautiful. They may have waterfalls, grand cathedral forests, or long vistas across spires of pure rock and desert. Or they may be buoyant with artifacts or ruins that carry the energy of ancient peoples. In any case, something about the majesty and physical being of the site lifts and stretches our inner awareness.

All we have to do is walk into the location, and if we exhibit even the slightest amount of openness, we begin to feel different, more than ourselves. We feel physically at one with everything around us and with the whole of creation, a sensation that fills us with inner security and well-being and wisdom.

Locating Sacred Sites

Most of us are familiar with the well-known mystical sites, such as Stonehenge, the Great Pyramids, the Grand Canyon, and Machu Picchu, but sacred sites do not have to be famous; they can be found in every state and county in the United States and throughout the world. Many have been mapped out by native peoples in their art and folklore. Others, however, have never been reported or documented in our time, and lie undisturbed in the few wilderness areas remaining in the world.

Because of this, they must be rediscovered by you and me—a search that I believe is already under way. In most cases, there is someone who at least intuits where these special places are, and who could serve as a potential protector. If you are unsure of where the special sites may be in your area, I would suggest checking first with your local senior citizens' groups or with elderly people you know. You will usually find a storehouse of information and sometimes testimony about the power of a local site. You might also be saddened by stories of special areas that have been carelessly destroyed by clear-cutting or mining or poorly planned construction projects.

Another way to locate these special sites is to visit your nearest state or national park or national forest and look around for yourself. Just beyond the first hill you may find a place of incredible power for you. Spend some time and test it out for yourself.

You might also want to be on guard for threats to these areas, for they are being destroyed at a rapid rate. Even on our public lands in the United States, Congress still allows multinational corporations to clear-cut some of our last remaining wilderness, beautiful areas containing trees that are hundreds of years old. Most citizens aren't aware of this ongoing system of corporate welfare at the cost of our children's heritage.

MEASURES OF THE MYSTICAL EXPERIENCE

As the synchronicity leads us to take the next step into direct mystical experience, we are all overcoming the temptation to merely intellectualize this journey. Loving the idea of mystical transformation, being intrigued by it, keeping it in mind, is great as a first step. But, as we all are coming to recognize, believing intellectually is not the same thing as actually living the experience.

I mention this again because the old materialistic paradigm constantly keeps us thinking and analyzing and relating to places and things from that perspective. No one, of course, is qualified to assess whether you yourself have experienced such an inner opening to the divine except you. That's why the experience has always been so elusive and mysterious. What we are seeking is more than just the intellectual appreciation of the beauty of a special site, or the comfortable relaxation of prayer and meditation, or the elation of success with a game.

We all must find that spiritual experience we have never felt before that expands our sense of self from within, transforming our understanding of who we are, opening us to the intelligence behind the universe. That's why very often we must wait until we have the experience itself to realize exactly what it consists of. Until then we have no real example of how we will be affected.

Still, I believe the expanding conversation about real

transcendent experience is helping in this regard. The mystics have always maintained that the experience of the absolute that can be described is not the real experience, and I believe this is true. On the other hand, there seem to be shared measures for such an experience that are emerging in human awareness that can guide us along the way and help us to decide whether the experience is really occurring.

THE SENSE OF LIGHTNESS

One of the measures we can apply is a sense of lightness. During a mystical experience, instead of having to struggle against gravity, pushing ourselves away from the earth with our feet as we stand up or walk, we begin to feel just the way we feel when we're on a fast elevator headed down. Our sense of being heavy decreases and we begin to acquire the sensation of almost floating.

This phenomenon seems to occur in all mystical experience, whether it occurs during prayer, meditation, dance, or any of the other pathways. We may be in a yogic posture or practicing tai ch'i or walking toward a site of great beauty when suddenly our sense of our bodies begins to change. We feel an energy that begins to fill us from within, and at the same time removes tightness and stress within our muscles. Our sense of movement shifts as well. Instead of moving with a sense of individual muscles pushing outward against the ground or floor, one's entire body begins to move from a central position in the torso.

When we stand up or walk, it takes less effort to move our legs and arms because the energy to do so now emanates from this central source. In fact, the power of that energy gives us the sense that we are hovering or floating over the ground. This explains why the movement disciplines of yoga, dance and the martial arts are so conducive to inner transcendence. They allow us to experience gravity in a new way, prying open the energy within, and when it comes in fully, we feel expanded to such a degree that our bodies begin to move into perfect posture. Our heads lift and extend to the full reach of our spines. Our backs feel stronger, erect of their own energy, rather than because of intentional muscular effort.

A sense of lightness, then, is a precise indication of a mystical experience. It is something we can measure; we know that as the transcendent is achieved, we begin to feel more buoyant, as though a channel of spiritual energy has begun to inflate us from within.

THE SENSE OF CLOSENESS AND CONNECTION

Another known shift in awareness that occurs during an inner transcendent experience concerns the degree of closeness we feel to the objects around us. By closeness,

I mean that everything suddenly appears nearer to us. This can occur during any of the mentioned pathways to the mystical, but its effect is heightened when we are in an area where we can see a long distance.

In this setting, a distant cloud floating in the sky suddenly becomes more pronounced in our awareness. Rather than being part of the flat background, without particular interest to our consciousness, the cloud now stands out with a new sense of form and presence. Suddenly, it feels closer to us, as if we could just reach up and touch it with an outstretched hand. In this state, other objects appear closer as well: a distant mountain, trees on the downslope, streams in the valley. All these objects now seem to have more presence and bearing even though they are far away. They literally jump out at us and demand attention.

Related to this perception is the common mystical description of having a sense of oneness with all things. As we look over our environment while in this consciousness, everything in our awareness seems to be a part of us, although not in the sense of relating to the things of the world by seeing through their eyes. Rather, as Alan Watts points out, this experience is one of sensing that everything around us is part of our larger, cosmic self, and is now seeing through our eyes.[6]

A SENSE OF SECURITY, ETERNITY, AND LOVE

We have already discussed the important findings of both the mystics and the depth psychologists—that humans tend to be insecure and anxious in the world, cut off from the inner source of their being. Life grasped with full existential awareness is often ominous and foreboding, with death always looming large. In the face of this anxiety, as we have seen, humanity has coped in two historic ways. One is that we have become unconscious and have pushed the reality of our insecurity far in the background by creating a rich culture with lots of activity and diversions and heroic meaning. This is why the modern age, for instance, threw itself into secular, material concerns, pushing away everything that reminded us of the mysteries of existence.

On a personal level, we further sought to resolve our insecurity by seeking to dominate other human beings, either passively or aggressively, and thus receiving what we now know to be spiritual energy from the other person, which made us feel temporarily fuller and more secure. The common control dramas are the ways most of us manipulate for this energy. Yet we must remember that it is because we are short of energy, cut off from the source, that the dramas operate.

It is this existential insecurity that the inner mystical opening resolves. Therefore, an uplifting sense of security and euphoria is a key measure for this state of being.

As we open up to the divine energy within, we experience a knowing that life is eternal and spiritual. This comes from the perception that we are personally part of the great order of the universe. Not only are we eternal but we are cared for, included in, even instrumental for the great plan that is life on earth. And if we closely attend the sense of well-being and security that flows into us, we can see that we feel secure, because we are filled with a strong emotion that pushes out all other emotion; we are imbued with a great sense of love.

Love, of course, is the best-known measure of inner transcendence. Yet this is a love different from the human love with which we are familiar. We all have experienced a kind of love that requires an object of focus: a parent, spouse, child, or friend. The love that is a measure of the transcendent opening is of another kind. It is a love that exists without an intended focus, and it becomes a pervasive constant that keeps our other emotions in perspective.

REMEMBERING OUR EXPERIENCES

I believe that these identifiable measures of transcendent experience are beneficial in two ways. First, they help us in our search for actual mystical experience. Not in advance, for we must let go of the intellect in order to enter into the transcendent; but afterward, as we assess whether we have, in fact, broken through to this level of awareness.

Second, the measures help us integrate this transcendent experience into our daily lives. Mystical experiences are fleeting at best and soon vanish as quickly as they begin. Afterward we must participate in the discipline of a practice, a way of regularly praying, meditating, moving, that is intended to return to and build upon the euphoria of the mystical state.

Each day we must remember how we felt, recalling each of the measures, and then embrace them, intend them, integrate them into our lives. As we'll discuss later, we can never completely succeed in pulling out of the control dramas we run into or in dealing with our own manipulations until we have enough energy and security within. This is what only the mystical experience can give us, and afterward we must remember the awareness we felt.

With our first move out of bed in the morning, we can remember the measures and thus move as close to the original consciousness as possible. Remember the lightness and coordination, the sense of closeness and oneness, the inflow of inner energy and security. Most important is that we remember the state of divine love we felt. Through practice, we can summon up the memory of the feeling, until we are filled with love to guide us through our day.

If this love is there, then we know we are open to the

divine source of energy that is always within us. This, of course, does not mean that we will never again feel the negative emotions of anger, jealousy, or hate. It only means that when we do, the constancy of love keeps those negative emotions from taking over our minds. They are put into a reasonable perspective in which we can feel them and let them go, focusing again on the pervasive love that energizes our being.

I believe we must again remind ourselves that only we, as individuals, can intend that these measures become a part of our everyday lives. After an experience of transcendence, we must engage the discipline to integrate them ourselves. When we are near others who exhibit such an awareness, we can be reminded, but there is no substitute for going back to the well, consciously, to increase the reflection of these measures in our personal lives.

When we make this disciplined commitment to maintain the energy opening that we have experienced, we begin to take the next step in awareness. We begin to notice an acceleration in the coincidences, for we are now becoming more aware of our own unique path of destiny.

7

DISCOVERING
WHO WE ARE

Once we find the transcendent experience and open up to a greater flow of spiritual energy and security within, something profound begins to occur. We begin to see ourselves and our behavior from a higher perspective, from the viewpoint of our more energized higher self. Our sense of identity moves past the insecure reactions of our ego self and assumes a witness viewpoint, identified now with all of divine creation and able to see our socially defined self with a new objectivity.

From this viewpoint, I believe one of our first clear observations is of how we personally react under stress. For the first time, we can see our own control drama with clarity. We could be anywhere when it happens: at work, at the market, perhaps engaging in a conversation with an important person in our lives. At first, we are living our new openness fully, but then something happens. The situation turns stressful, and we find ourselves reverting to our old drama.

We struggle to maintain our higher-self energy, to keep that witness position, even as a part of ourselves continues the defensive behavior. Here we may have a sense of revelation about ourselves when we watch our actions. Old comments from others about our patterns and scripts, comments we may have vehemently denied at the time, can surface again with a new sense of validity. We might even want to say, "So this is how I really act when under pressure."

We may be seeing the guilt-tripping actions of a Poor Me, the distancing of an Aloof, the criticisms of an Interrogator, or the fear-producing posture of an Intimidator. Regardless, we have the experience of fully seeing our own manipulations for other people's energy.

POWER STRUGGLES
IN THE EARLY FAMILY

Now the question becomes: Where did our behavior originate? And what can we do about it?

Such questioning sends us to the groundbreaking research on family dynamics done in the 1960s and 1970s. We know that the family, especially parents, structures our first exposure to the world. (If our parents are not present, there are other caretakers who serve in the same role.) These people teach us, as we model their attitudes and behavior, our first idea of what the world is about.

As psychologist James Hillman makes clear in his recent book *The Soul's Code,*[1] we all come in with character and calling. But the fog of birth obscures this self-understanding, and the struggles of childhood can often be intense and very fearful. As children we lose our sure connection with divine love and energy. We are suddenly dependent for food and protection and security.

Too often, we receive too little love and energy because our caretakers have too little to give and are operating from control dramas themselves. Some parents unconsciously drain the energy of their young children, forcing them to mold dramas of their own in order to fight back. For instance, a Poor Me might constantly shame his child for not helping enough, or even blame the child for his problems, saying something like, "If it weren't for you, I could go on with my career." The Aloof parent would be distant, implying conditional love. An Interrogator would constantly find fault. And an Intimidator would create a climate of fear.

As children we would first buy into the dramas, allowing our energy to be depleted. But at a certain point, our defenses would be stimulated and we would begin to develop our own maneuvers to stop the loss of energy and self-esteem. Toward the Poor Me and the Aloof, we usually develop an Interrogator's stance, fighting off the guilt trip or ending the distancing with a criticism of some characteristic or behavior we found in them. Toward an Interrogator, we might interrogate in return or adopt the Aloof's facade of indifference.

The case of the Intimidator is more complex. When the childhood situation is abusive and frightful, most respond at first with a Poor Me drama. If the Intimidator responds to the guilt trip and begins to give energy back, it stops there. But if the Poor Me posture doesn't work, the only recourse to the life-threatening theft of our energy is to explode into intimidation ourselves as children—sometimes against the ones who are trying to intimidate us, but just as often against siblings and others who are smaller or less powerful.[2]

THE LIBERATION OF FORGIVENESS

Buoyed by our present higher energy level, we now face a challenge to our continued evolution. Once we look closely at the dynamics of our early family, traumatic as they may be, we must avoid the tendency to blame and hate. As we shall see later, our advancing consciousness is leading us ultimately to see all that has happened in our lives from the perspective of the Afterlife dimension, wherein we know that at our highest connection with the divine, we chose the circumstances we were born into. We may have intended that it come out differently, but we wanted to begin our lives just as we did.

If we find ourselves hanging on to the need to blame parents or siblings or anyone else in our early lives, it is usually because blame itself is a part of our control drama. We tell the tale of our abuse to win sympathy or energy, or we use it to rationalize our Aloof or Interrogator strategies. This is why we cannot fully pursue an inner energy connection with the divine until we free ourselves of our past. We can't go forward and continue to expand our energy because blame always throws us back into the old drama.

Only forgiveness can fully liberate our potential to go past these repeated scripts that waste our time. And I believe that forgiveness must be expressed and demonstrated to be totally freeing. Many therapists recommend that we write a letter to everyone that we blame offering our forgiveness. That doesn't mean we have to spend any time with this person; such acts just create closure and clear the air for a new life to begin. Forgiveness reinforces the higher witness awareness that we have acquired. The key to forgiveness is simply acknowledging that everyone was doing the best he or she could at the time.[3]

RELEASING OUR
CONTROL DRAMA

This is the point at which our control drama can be effectively released. If we proceed with a certain amount of discipline, transcending the old attitudes about the past that keep us locked into a pattern of responses, we can begin to fully integrate our new spiritual self and let the other socially defined identity go.

In this state of awareness, we can more readily maintain a witness position on our own behavior and life path, watching the events that happen with a sense of objective faith and love of adventure. This is the position from which we can best understand and follow the messages of the coincidences, and it is the position from which we can best stay alert, even under the most stressful of situations.

Consider this scenario: We are attempting to stay in our higher-self state when suddenly someone comes along and does something that spontaneously puts us on the defensive. If our control drama is that of the Interrogator, the person might remind us of the Aloofs or Poor Me's in our past and so elicit the same critical response. Our eyes might immediately go to a fault we noticed in the person and attack him there, intending to throw him off balance and to make sure his Aloof or Poor Me responses don't drain us.

In that moment, we have moved out of our higher-self position and into a place of insecurity again, needing the energy of others. To reduce and then stop these moments of unconscious defensiveness, we must catch ourselves earlier and earlier. This in itself takes intention and is helped by a commitment to a spiritual practice of meditation or prayer. Once we have worked to maintain our higher-self position with discipline, however, and have seen the way our unique control drama takes form, we must stay alert, with intention, in order to spot the first signs of a control drama popping up again.

Once we can catch ourselves every time, we have begun to break the pattern, to stop the drama before it begins, and to hang on to our higher-self witness position on a constant basis.

INTUITING A GREATER PURPOSE FOR OUR LIVES

Once we are maintaining our higher-self posture most of the time, the increased energy and sense of freedom immediately bring up other questions: If we are not that person who creates a repetitive drama in our lives as a defense, then what are our lives about? What should we be doing?

I believe these questions come directly from a particular characteristic of the higher-self connection, which is an inner sense that each of us has of what our lives are meant to accomplish. It is this intuition that creates a need to understand our possible destiny from a higher perspective. This includes a prevailing need to reinterpret our past.

What were our ancestors like? Where did they live and how did they spend their lives? Eventually, our focus lands again on our parents and early family, and here is where our commitment to forgiveness can fully pay off, for now we can move past the old resentments to consider that experience with an objective eye.

I believe the real question concerning our early family experience should be this: Why would I have chosen to be born in this place and to this cast of characters? What could I have possibly had in mind?

THE MESSAGE OF THE EARLY FAMILY

The purpose behind such a question is to find a higher understanding of our experience with our family of origin. Remember, our early family was the environment in which each of us first learned what the world was like and what was expected of us as human beings. A child must learn everything, not just the name of every object in the universe, but the meaning that these objects have in human life. To learn this, we had to watch closely how our parents or caretakers interpreted this vast world. This means we spend the first decade of life looking at the world through the eyes of our parents to see their descriptions, emotional reactions, and creativity. And as we have seen, this identification shapes and structures our initial worldview.

To find the spiritual reason we were born to our parents, we must look very deeply at who they were, how they viewed the world, and perhaps more important, at their dreams, both realized and unrealized.

SEEING OUR MOTHERS

For most of us, the touch and love we felt from our mothers created our first inner description of the world. Was it responsive, nurturing, good? Or was it neglectful and ominous?

Psychologists tell us that the first five years of life establish the basic assumptions we have about whether the world will meet our needs and whether we can trust that our experiences will be positive. If it appears that our mothers met our needs, then we should have a basically positive view. But what if we don't? What if our early nurturing seemed very positive but we still find ourselves, in anxious moments, fighting against an inner negativism or fear? If this is the case, we must consider that the negative imprint comes from an even earlier time in our existence—difficulty at birth, for instance, or even in a past life.

I realize that many people are unsure of the reality of past lives. If you have this skepticism, I would suggest you read the work of Dr. Brian Weiss, the psychiatrist whose casework and documentation of past-life memories in his patients has popularized and clarified this phenomenon throughout the world.[4] In many cases, as we reevaluate the effect of our early situation on our attitudes and life direction, we have to include the possibility that some of our assumptions come from a past existence.

Your mother, of course, brought more to you than this first imprint of nurturing. She also conveyed a specific and sometimes unique interpretation of the world. To understand your mother's viewpoint, you must see her as fully as possible, taking the time to look at her parents, at the cultural conditioning she experienced in her youth, and at the way this climate restricted or liberated her dream of who she wanted to be.

For most of us, our mothers came of age sometime between the 1940s and the 1980s, a time of shifting possibilities for women. The experience of working in factories and defense plants during World War II, for instance, holding jobs formerly held only by men, changed the attitude about women's potential around the world. Yet individual women, in individual family settings, suffered varying degrees of restrictions on their aspirations, and it is for this reason that you must look closely at your mother's life.

What were the values she expressed about life, fam-

ily, work? How did this differ from the prevailing sentiment in your community? As you watched her grow
older, what was her attitude toward health, healing, the
inner spiritual life? At the level of her highest self, what
was her vision for how she thought human beings
should live? And how well was she able to actualize this
vision?

Equally important is to look at how you felt as a child
about your mother's dreams. Did you intuitively think
she was right or wrong in her values and outlook? What
do you think about it now that forgiveness has cleared
the air and you're past your youthful rebellion?

Most important of all, in my opinion, is your higher-
self intuitive analysis right now, in the present, of your
mother's overall life. If you could change what happened, adjust her decisions, in what way would you do
so? And lastly, how did watching her life, both as a child
and subsequently, influence the way you have decided
to live your own life?

SEEING OUR FATHERS

The analysis of our fathers should follow the same process. You can look closely at how your father approached life, especially how he related to other people
and felt about spiritual issues. What stood out as a philosophy that worked for him? What skills did you learn

through example? What was his dream for himself, and in what ways did he succeed or fail in achieving it?

Remember that he helped to instill in you, whether you like it or not, half your general framework for reality, including how you act in the world, deal with business associates and partners, negotiate and honor various contracts, and create income. Overall you were shown a specific wisdom and prejudice, and you must ask yourself why you wanted to see this particular angle on life at the very beginning of your existence. What issues did you want to be immediately sensitized to?

As with your mother, you must analyze your intuitive reaction to your father. What part of his life, world, dreams, and style did you agree with? What parts did you think were in error? Did you, and do you still, consider your father's life a success or a failure? And how, from your viewpoint now, would you change his decisions and his overall course in life, if you could?

MERGING THE REALITIES

Once we see our parents' lives in a meaningful way, we often find that we were born to two very different people, with very different worldviews, interests, and values. What does it mean that we were socialized by both these people? Undoubtedly, we saw certain conflicts that arose as our parents themselves tried to reconcile their divergent views. As their children we have a unique understanding of this reconciliation. We grew up in a position between two unique people, and we integrated both ways of being during our socialization process.[5]

Our challenge is to find a synthesis of our parents' perspectives, one that points to a more truthful existence. In my own case, my father always wanted to see the world as positive and fun, the home of great adventure. His was a secular world, devoid of a lived spirituality, and often his search for fun led him into decisions that blew up or backfired. As I grew up, I saw this pattern and was sensitized to the need for a more strategic approach to adventure. My mother, on the other hand, knew the world to be deeply spiritual, but it was a pious and self-denying spirituality. She sacrificed any idea of personal adventure for the hard work of helping others and solving the world's ills.

What did it mean that I was born between these two people? Their own reconciliation was difficult. My mother always wanted to domesticate my father and put him to work in spiritual service. He always rebelled, intuiting that life was about expanding one's horizons, although he wasn't quite sure how to pull that off. As I stepped back and looked at this situation, I saw the obvious solution. One could pursue life with the deep spirituality held by my mother, which included making the world better, but it could be a fun and adventurous pursuit, wherein one's mission was also the exact place one could find the deepest inspiration. I realized that understanding higher spirituality was my basic life question.

This synthesis of my parents' lives and the best of their viewpoints also gave me the sense that I was completing their life purposes in some way and helping them to evolve in the present. Most interesting of all, I discovered that this synthesis of their views fit exactly with how I intuitively wanted to live my life, as though my experience with them was simply intended to wake me up to it.

THE PROGRESS OF THE GENERATIONS

To some degree, the new spiritual awareness is emerging because more and more of us are discovering a personal interpretation of our early family situation. At an intuitive level, this was what propelled our mass entry into therapy in the 1970s. We knew that our awareness expands when we review our early family life. Now we are expanding our search further, fully grasping that it was no accident that we were born to our parents and no mere act of chance that their wisdom and still incomplete approaches to life were exactly the stimulation we needed in order to find our own viewpoint and to discover the direction we desired for our lives.

In this sense, as we shall discuss in later sections of this book, each generation, to whatever degree it is centered in spiritual truth, expands and evolves the worldview of the previous one. This is how we participate in the continuing flow of evolution that so many thinkers have now identified. All we are doing is making the process more conscious.

FRIENDS, EDUCATION, AND EARLY EMPLOYMENT

Of course, our early family experience was only the beginning. As youths, we quickly moved forward in our own direction. Think, for instance, about all the other influences during childhood, beginning with our siblings. How did we feel about our brothers and sisters? What did we learn? Why did certain people attract our attention and others repel us? Why did we choose certain friends and ignore others? And why did these choices occur precisely when they did?

What about the teachers we chose as favorites? Each of us had particular mentors whose views or attitudes attracted us, and as a result we considered their outlooks and their subject matter much more seriously, often lingering after class for personal discussions and learning at a deeper level. Why those particular teachers, at that particular time? What talents did they help us identify?

Just as significant are the other educational choices we made. What were our early interests and fantasies about what we wanted to do with our lives? What were the classes and topics that we loved? What field did we discover that we could be good at?

Another important development in our past was the early employment opportunities that came our way. What kind of jobs did we take as students or later as young adults? How did these jobs influence us by clarifying what we wanted to do?

The purpose of this review is to find a higher synchronistic meaning for the course your life has taken. Beginning with the idea that each of us reconciles and, to some degree, completes our parents' unfulfilled promise, we can discover even greater clarity by noticing the area of human life and knowledge we seemed to have been drawn toward as our lives evolved. Friends and teachers offered us additional perspectives and lifestyles that we could learn from and integrate into our unique self.

WHAT HAVE WE BEEN PREPARED TO DO?

By inspecting this personal evolution, we can find the most truthful way of understanding our childhood and life story from the very beginning all the way up to the present moment. The pieces will continue to fall into place throughout your life, but right now you can look back at all that has happened and ask yourself: From the influence of my early family through all the synchronistic twists and turns, the dead ends, mistakes, and successes, what, as a result of all these events, was I being prepared to tell the world? What particular truth, unique to myself and my experience, can I now go out and convey to others about how one can live life more fully and spiritually?

This is the meaning that can emerge from a Life Review. We can get a sense of what we stand for, what attitudes we want to convey that express our message to others. The truth we have to share does not have to be complicated and large. Sometimes the most important truths are the smallest and simplest. The essential point, in my opinion, is that we understand what our truth is at the current moment and be ready to express it with courage, whenever appropriate. We will find that those who cross our path are there to hear our truth. No matter how small you think your truth is, its impact can be large and global depending on whom you influence and how it serves to clarify others' truths and what they go on to do in the world.

THE EVOLUTION OF
OUR TRUTHS

Our truths are always evolving, not in sporadic or unde-
fined ways, but precisely and clearly, as we follow the
synchronicity in our lives. What usually comes up is the
question of what to do with our truths, how we might
tell it to others. Should our truth be something we develop as a career, or is it more fitting to do something
else and let the telling of our truths be our avocation?

Of utmost importance is to reality-check our truths
with others and pay attention not just to those who
agree. Out of an honest conversation will emerge the
best description of reality. A truth about a more fulfilling
way to approach life can be ineffective if it is expressed
in a form that is too complicated or offered as a philosophy for which others have no frame of reference. It is
also important to realize that our truths do not have to
be spiritual in nature. Certainly, they will be about moving human understanding toward the spiritual. But they
will apply to the particular field in which we already
work or have influence. One truth might be about resolving conflicts. Another might be a new approach in
computer technology that liberates humanity in some
way.

One thing of which we can be sure: If we pay attention, if we stay focused on our truths and continue to
keep our energy high, we will find to our delight that
the coincidences will begin to escalate and become more
meaningful than ever.

8

EVOLVING
CONSCIOUSLY

Here, perhaps, we should review the new spiritual awareness that we have discussed. We began with the reality of coincidences, emphasizing that they always seem to be pulling us toward some special destiny.

The second step was to overcome the inertia of the old worldview by understanding the psychology of why we denied the mysteries of existence for so long. We can appreciate humanity's materialistic accomplishments but recognize that the world is about so much more and that it is time to move forward, certain that our blossoming spiritual perception represents an awakening of great historical significance.

We integrate the third step when we truly begin to grasp, every day, that we live in a mysterious, energy-dynamic universe that responds to our intentions and assumptions.

This sets the stage for the fourth step, which is to learn to negotiate this spiritual world, especially the reality of human insecurity and the competition for energy. Each of us must solve this problem of insecurity individually, by discovering for ourselves the transcendent experience described by the mystics of all ages, which is the fifth step. This is an experience that gives us a glimpse of higher consciousness and opens an inner connection that we can remember and go back to, as we work to keep our energy high and our security based within.

Once we open to the divine source of energy, we can enter the sixth step and experience the spiritual catharsis of dropping our control drama and discovering who we really are, achieving finally an understanding of a truth about the world that is ours to tell. At this point, we can live with a fuller awareness within which we are ever more alert to synchronicity and engage more fully in our destiny.

EXPANDING OUR PERCEPTION

We are now ready for the seventh step. This involves learning to follow the coincidences with greater skill.

Let's look again at an example of a synchronistic experience. Suppose you attend a lecture on a subject of interest to you, and sitting there listening to the speaker, you think, "This person has a fascinating angle on his topic. I need to understand more about his perspective." Then you go out to dinner that night and find yourself seated at a table right beside the person who gave the speech, sitting alone.

Obviously, you have just experienced a meaningful coincidence. Yet in reality this synchronicity began long before that night. Why, for instance, did you decide to attend that lecture in the first place? How did you hear about it? Perhaps you saw an ad as you were glancing through the paper. Yet what moved you to actually attend? Why did this particular synchronicity occur?

DISCERNING OUR LIFE QUESTION

Even after we initially perceive it, our understanding of the truth we are here to tell is always in a state of evolution, always moving into clearer form. We might have found, for example, that a love and reverence for plants has characterized our past and that conveying the message that we should protect plant life is the basic truth we have to tell. After this revelation, however, we always want more detail. Should I continue my education? Should I leave my current employment and look for something more relevant to plants?

As we pay attention to our increased awareness, the question most relevant to our life situation will make itself known. Sometimes we will discover that question spontaneously. At other times, the nature of the coincidences occurring around us will help define the question. Let's suppose, for instance, that the lecture you attended was about efforts to save the few old-growth, virgin forests left in America, and the speaker talked about the most effective, nonprofit organizations in this effort and the employment opportunities available.

While one such occurrence isn't conclusive, a series of coincidences hinting at employment considerations might mean that this is the most pressing question. In our hypothetical example, the fact that the speaker is now sitting right beside you in the restaurant would be such a confirming synchronicity.

Always when interpreting the coincidences in our lives, we must begin by first discerning the life question most pressing for us. This question will point us in the direction our truth is evolving and make the meaning of any one synchronicity more easily apparent to us.

INTUITION

What happens after we discern a life question? How did you recognize that you should attend that particular lecture? What happened? Upon closer inspection, I believe we are recognizing and beginning to fully use an age-old human ability: our intuition.

Throughout history, humans have always talked about the experience of gut feelings or hunches that have directed us at various times in the decisions we make in life. Only the mechanistic worldview discounted such experiences as illusion or hallucination or reduced them to mere social cues.[1] Even in the face of this cultural disapproval, most of us have continued to use such feelings half-consciously; we just didn't discuss them much. Only in recent decades has the power of intuition once again become more openly used and talked about in the West.

I believe that our challenge now is to pull these subtle feelings more fully into awareness and to learn to distinguish them from ordinary thoughts. Since this ability is a question of internal perception, we each must work it out by ourselves. But the general pattern of how our intuition operates may already be reaching the level of consensus for many of us.

An intuition is an image of an occurrence in the future, a precognition that has been scientifically demonstrated to be a human ability.[2] It may concern ourselves or others. Almost always, this image is of a positive, growthful nature. If, on the other hand, these thoughts are negative—of an impending accident or of a place to be avoided, for example—then we have to decide whether we are merely having fear thoughts that come from a repeated control drama or whether the negative image is a true intuitive warning.

Again, making the distinction between the two is

something each of us must work out for ourselves, but I think we can see that fear images usually have to do with generalized fears and not specific events. In the case of our example, we might know that we have always feared going to lectures if, say, we had to go alone. That kind of fear, as it comes up again and again, can usually be recognized as a general fear. But if we spontaneously feel fear about a particular lecture, when we have had no such fear before, then such an image might be a true intuitive warning of some kind, and we should act on it accordingly.

We must also distinguish an intuition from a dysfunctional daydream. If we are imagining a replay of a previous social interaction in our minds, wishing we had voiced a powerful comeback to someone who angered or upset us, we are merely fantasizing a control game in our head. This kind of image is useful only if the message is to give up such competitions.[3]

Most real intuitions involve the picture of some future action on our part that would move our lives in an advantageous new direction, and they always carry a charge of inspiration around them.

THE PROCESS OF SYNCHRONICITY

Now we have a broader view of synchronicity. It begins with our life question, conscious or not, and moves forward. In the case of our example, you have discerned that your question is whether you should pursue different employment, something more closely related to plants.

At this point, our intuition comes into play. If we pay close attention to our thoughts, we will receive an intuition about what to do or where to go. It could be very vague and confusing, but it will be a true precognition of a potential event in the future. In our example, you might receive an actual image of being at a lecture. Or perhaps it would be a more general picture of just receiving information about a plant-related business or employment opportunity.

After that, when you open the newspaper and read about the coming lecture on plants, a lightbulb would go off in your mind. You would recognize immediately that you are having a synchronistic moment, oozing in inspiration. When you arrive at the event and hear the speech, you would receive even more validation. And finding the speaker next to your table at dinner that night would be almost unbelievable.

In summary, we can see that most synchronicities occur in the following way: We start with a background sense of the truth we are here to tell, a truth that is becoming ever more clear and manifests first in the form of our prime question, and then in the question most urgent in our current life situation. Afterward comes an intuition, a mental image of something happening, of ourselves taking some sort of action in order to pursue the answer to this question. If we pay attention, an actual opportunity approximating our intuition will occur, bringing in answers and feeling perfectly synchronistic.

These answers, of course, while resolving our first question, will always lead us forward into a new life situation and more questions. And so the process continues: question, intuition, synchronistic answer, new question.

DREAMS

As we explored earlier, dreams can play an important role in this process, because dreams are an obscured form of intuition. While in most cases the images in a dream involve strange characters and unlikely plots, almost always the elements can bring insight to our current situation. In Chapter 2, we discussed how to analyze the plot of a dream and then superimpose this plot on the larger story going on in our lives. Always, we can see some relationship, either now or in the future.[4]

If the dream is about fighting, for instance, we can look to see whether we are, in some sense, fighting some development in our actual lives. If this is true, the dream might be pointing out a better course, one that has not yet come to mind. This new course of action, once pursued, might lead to life-changing synchronicities, just as an intuition does.

The key in interpreting dreams in this manner is to always have our basic truth and our current question forefront in our minds. Keeping these concerns in our consciousness helps give us additional information with which to look for meaning. We need to ask ourselves: How does the story of the dream relate to the questions we face in our lives?

LUMINOSITY

Another way our intuitions can be enhanced is through luminosity. Luminosity refers to the phenomenon of experiencing a certain place or object that seems to stand out, attracting our attention. The place or object seems to have more presence than whatever is near it.[5]

In the case of a landscape, the colors of the trees and rocks and earth seem more radiant. This experience is related to the transcendental moment in which everything around us suddenly becomes alive with presence and being and seems to become as connected to us as our own bodies, producing a sense of oneness—except that in the case of luminosity, the phenomenon is isolated to one specific area, as if to show us a special connection we have with the object or setting in question.

Very often such an experience of luminosity occurs when we are making a decision about which direction to take when on a journey. This, of course, challenges the old secular paradigm—because our habit is to make decisions about particular routes based on time considerations, maps, and other logical considerations. And certainly, these methods have in the past proved effective in getting us to a specific location.

But as we expand beyond this logical way of running our lives by learning to use intuition in our decision-making process, we can be more efficient in the long run. Intuition might guide us to take a route that is geographically longer or more difficult, but along that journey may come life-enhancing information that would have taken much longer to come to us if we had pursued our journey solely by the old method.

Often all we know is that a certain route seems vaguely more attractive. A good check on this kind of feeling is to look at the other routes and compare their luminosity to the one that seems to be calling us. Do we get the same feeling? Does the light seem different? Each person must validate such perceptions for himself, but if the route still seems more attractive, take it.

Another way that luminosity can help guide our path is when we are exploring a sacred site in search of the areas of greatest energy. Sacred sites, as we have already discussed, often facilitate mystical or transcendental experiences during which we open channels of divine energy within. Often we must discover the best sites intuitively. Sometimes we have little to go on besides rumor or vague comments we've heard somewhere. The key to our successful search can often be one using luminosity.

This is especially true if we are in a wilderness area,

where the expanse of acreage is vast. In such settings, if we look around, sensitive to what stands out to us, we'll often notice a mountain peak in the distance, a group of large trees, or areas with water that seem especially brilliant and inwardly attractive to us. Once we make our way there, we can use the same process to find an even more specific location that seems to stand out and feel inviting and comfortable. This is the place to meditate.

CHOOSING OUR SEATING IN A PUBLIC PLACE

Intuition and luminosity also work well in helping us choose a seat at a restaurant or meeting, for example, especially in those instances where we will be interacting with other people. When entering such a space, if we pay close attention, one place or another will stand out and become luminous. We may have to negotiate with the hostess at a restaurant, who usually has her own idea of where we should sit. But it's worth the effort, as the right place will give us a sense of comfort and excitement.

At worst, choosing our seating in this manner will lead to a pleasant meal, given the energy configuration of the room and the dispersal of people. At best, it could lead to an important synchronistic encounter. Many times, such a process has led me to a synchronistic conversation. At the time I was writing this chapter, I experienced just this kind of synchronicity at a local restaurant.

Earlier that day, I met a man who was jogging near my home. We spoke briefly and he told me about an experimental air ionizer and filter that he had heard about. I was short on time, so I didn't ask him any details, but later I lamented not getting more information from him, because I realized the kind of ionizer he was describing could help me with some work I was doing. Since I had no apparent way of contacting the jogger, I forgot all about it and drove into town for breakfast. As I entered Irene's Cafe, I looked around and was immediately drawn to a table near a window on the right. The waitress wanted me to sit in another section, but the light virtually glowed around this particular table.

A group of people were talking at the table next to it, but I didn't notice much about them; my focus was on the table I had chosen. With a smile, the waitress allowed me to sit down and I settled in and picked up the menu. Again, I paid little attention to the people sitting at the next table. Then I heard a voice I seemed to recognize and glanced to my right. There, having breakfast with some friends, was the jogger I had been talking to about the ionizer.

Needless to say, we finished our conversation in depth, and it turned out to be very meaningful to my work.

BOOKS, MAGAZINES,
AND THE MEDIA

Luminosity also points out useful information in the form of books, magazines, and television programs. One hears many stories, for example, about the way books mysteriously appear in people's lives. Shirley MacLaine shared a common version of this experience in *Out on a Limb,* where she tells the story of being at the Bodhi Tree bookstore in Los Angeles when a book she needed to read at the moment literally dropped off a top shelf into her lap.[6]

Almost as common is the story about how a book suddenly seems luminous and attractive. In fact, I believe anyone who is increasing his or her spiritual awareness will at times have this experience. We might enter a bookstore merely to browse and a particular book attracts our attention, sometimes from as far away as across the room. Somehow it seems brighter, more distinct. Sometimes we can read the title and author's name, when such perception would seem impossible at that distance.[7]

This experience, of course, is not limited to books. Magazines and certain television programs can also appear luminous. If we stay aware when we gaze at a shelf of magazines, very often we will notice certain ones standing out. A closer inspection will usually yield a particular story or editorial that contains synchronistic information.

We can watch television in exactly the same way. With the explosion of cable and satellite channels available now, we will often find ourselves clicking through them all, not sure what we are looking for. Yet if we keep the phenomenon of luminosity in mind, almost always something will catch our eye and then our interest.

WATCHING WHERE
OUR EYES FALL

Sometimes we will notice that our eyes spontaneously fall on a particular person, place, or object. If we listen closely, we can detect comments about this phenomenon in current discussions about spirituality. Friends will comment that their eyes spontaneously fell on a path through a forest or on a particular magazine or book. This is slightly different from luminosity. In this case, our eyes and minds seem to spontaneously focus somewhere while we are thinking about something else.

Spontaneously turning around and catching someone looking at us is a common example of this experience. In any of these cases, we may ask ourselves afterward: Why did I glance up just at that moment, or why was I looking at that building or park?

While these messages from our bodies may at first seem capricious, sometimes we will have an intuition to explore further. Often, just a few minutes of attentive action will lead to a new adventure or synchronistic encounter.

THE IMPORTANCE OF STAYING POSITIVE

I can't overemphasize the importance of keeping a positive outlook as our experiences of synchronicity increase. Once we have opened to the divine energy within and found a truth that inspires us, and kept our questions in mind, the flow of synchronicity accelerates and becomes easier to interpret. But at any point we can shift into a negative interpretation and lose our energy.

As I mentioned earlier, many times as I worked on *The Celestine Prophecy,* I found myself in what could only be called a dead end. I had been in a flow of synchronicity that was rich and meaningful, and then—boom—something would happen that suggested to me that I had been on the wrong path all along. At such times, I was tempted to abandon the project completely. I couldn't understand why what I thought I was supposed to be doing had fallen apart.

These dead ends continued to occur until I realized that I was jumping to negative conclusions just because I didn't want the project to be slowed down. Each of us has to realize, on our own, that at our higher level of awareness there are no negative events. Certainly, life can be tragic at times and humans often perpetrate evil, sometimes extreme evil. But at the level of personal growth and meaning, as Victor Frankl discussed in his classic book *Man's Search for Meaning,*[8] negativity represents only challenge, and in the worst of situations there is always an opportunity for growth. Each crisis, each dead end in our evolution, is merely a message, an opportunity to go in a different direction. Our egos might not like the direction at first, but our higher self can discover a new plan implicit in the challenge.

The importance of looking for the positive meaning in negative events cannot be overstated. Many times I have seen individuals begin the synchronistic path, successfully entering their journey into self-awareness and growth, only to encounter a dead end that they interpret negatively, causing them to give up on the whole process.

This occurs when we assume we can reach our most far-reaching goals and images very quickly. If we do not achieve these goals according to our timetable, we assume the negative and either blame ourselves or others in some way, or think that the whole process is invalid. In truth, a dead end usually points out that we are still short of energy or have not fully cleared our control drama. The synchronicity in our lives works to help us return to the issues of personal clearing and the need to discover a posture of love and inner security. Only by retrieving this transcendent space can we be free of ego needs and proceed to an objective reading of the coincidences.

EVOLVING STRATEGICALLY

We must be mindful that the new spiritual awareness we have been discussing is a balance between our rational and intuitive selves. We aren't discarding our hard-won powers of rational discernment; rather, we are bringing them into balance with the higher part of our being. In this way, we are entering a universe that provides a constant stream of little miracles to guide our way.

The key is to make sure we stay open to the synchronistic flow without jumping to conclusions too quickly. Every mysterious event in our lives is a message. If we keep our energy high and remember the truth we are here to tell, the process of synchronicity will continue—perhaps not as quickly as we would like, but it will continue. From our current questions will rise intuitive images of what we can do, and when we begin to take this action, exploring as we go, our flow will always move forward.

Our full engagement of the synchronistic process brings us immediately to the next step in living the new spiritual awareness. We will find that most synchronicity comes to us via the truths of other human beings. When we learn to interact with this realization in mind, we can all raise the process of spiritual evolution to a higher level.

9

LIVING THE NEW INTERPERSONAL ETHIC

One effect of the explosion of mass media, as Marshall McLuhan showed in his landmark book *The Medium Is the Message,*[1] has been to reduce the psychological vastness of the earth. Because of television, radio, and computerization, the world now seems smaller than ever before in human history. With just a flick of the dial, we can witness events as they happen, halfway around the globe.

At the local level, the effect of this global conversation is to make our interpretation of words and phrases, even across various languages, much more accurate. As our world becomes smaller, we are becoming homogenized and deepening our understanding of each other.

Little more than one human lifetime ago—a mere 120 years—dueling was legal in some parts of the

United States. Slights of honor were often the result of a slip of the tongue or the use of an expression that elsewhere in the country was perfectly acceptable, but in another region was grounds for committing a form of murder.

Mistakes of this kind are becoming more and more rare because across subcultures and regions we understand each other more clearly than ever before. Critics might bemoan television's erosion of many of our regional differences—and our loss of diversity is a problem—but modern media have also shown us ourselves, and in doing so have brought us closer together. As we homogenize the meaning of the words we use across the United States, and to some extent across the world, we are entering each other's minds as never before, deepening our dialogue and increasing the frequency of synchronicity.

THE SPIRITUALITY OF EVERYDAY CONVERSATION

Most synchronistic messages come from other people. A popular spiritual adage states: When the pupil is ready, the teacher will come. A more modern expression of this idea might be: If we are open and alert, someone will show up with a timely truth we need to hear. The key to receiving the information is to never fail to explore these encounters, taking, of course, reasonable precautions for safety.

A coincidental crossing of paths can occur at any time, but it usually won't happen unless we are willing to take the initiative ourselves. For instance, in the preceding chapter, we postulated that you had intuited the idea of going to a lecture about plants and discovered information about employment in the field. After the lecture, you synchronistically ran into the speaker over dinner.

Now what? How many times does a coincidental meeting take place and one or both parties fail to take advantage of it? Too often. But I believe our increased ability to understand each other is helping to reverse the situation. As more of us realize the truth of the evolutionary process, we will give ever more priority to sharing our personal truth with each other.

Let's look again at you sitting beside the lecturer at the restaurant. Since the synchronicity of the meeting has occurred, the next logical step is to express—in the most honest and revealing, yet nonthreatening, way possible—what is happening. You might get right to the point by saying, "I heard your lecture today and found it very interesting, because I'm thinking about pursuing a career in helping to save endangered plants."

In response, the lecturer might say something that provides you with another lead, such as, "I keep up with the growing opportunities in the field with a newsletter called *Botanical Update*." No doubt you would follow up a conversation like this by obtaining a copy of the newsletter, which, most probably, would contain even more information.

THE IMPORTANCE OF UPLIFTING OTHERS

But what if, after finding ourselves in a synchronistic meeting with another person, no messages immediately come to the surface—or, more likely, the messages are blocked by fear or a control drama of some kind? First of all, we can go within and try to increase our own energy level by focusing on love, lightness, and connection with the environment.

From this higher energy state, we can look with fresh eyes at the person with whom we've been talking. As we discussed in an earlier chapter, when confronting a control drama, we must first send loving energy to the person by focusing on him completely. What we are actually doing is sending spiritual energy to the higher self of the person; that allows him to ease the rigid assumptions defined by his control drama.

The mystical traditions tell us this is done in a special way.[2] A face, with its features, contours, and shadows, is much like an inkblot, the kind used in psychological tests. In a like way, we can see many expressions in a face, depending on our own attitude. If in our control drama we expect everyone we meet to be intimidating, or foolish, or neglectful, then that is the look that we will find. In fact, the person we're speaking to will usually begin to feel that way, perhaps even speaking threateningly or foolishly or thoughtlessly, reporting later that he seemed to be cast in that role in the conversation.

Remember that the universe responds to our intentions. Our thoughts and beliefs go out like prayers into the world, and the environment tries to give us what we seem to want. The key is to keep our energy high and to use the power of our intentions in a positive way.

But how, precisely, can we accomplish this? How do we apply this new focus to another human being? When we look at another's face now, what do we focus upon?

The answer, of course, is that we must focus on the wholeness of the other's face with an attitude of openness. As the other person talks, if we look closely, we can begin to see the higher self of that person, the particular expression that reflects the individual's greater awareness and knowledge. This idea is expressed in various religious traditions as seeing the glory on another's face, or the Christ, or the genius. However we express it, if we begin to speak to this higher self, this genius, projecting love at the same time, the person will begin to move into that awareness while we are interacting with him, perhaps feeling it for the first time.

This is the process of uplifting others in which we can now engage consciously. I believe more and more of us are using this process as a higher, ethical stance toward others. We have known for thousands of years that it is important to love one another and that transformative outcomes can be the result. Now we are learning and integrating the spiritual details of how to send this love.

What's crucial is that we understand that loving others is not just a question of being nice. There is a precise, psychological method to loving others that must be engaged in with specific intention and focus. And yet this ethic is entirely selfish, because if we practice it, we always get more out of the encounter than we put into it. When we strive to uplift others, they move closer to their higher-self knowledge and sense of purpose. And in doing so, they often bring up a subject—be it a project, solution, or plan—that provides us with a synchronistic message, perhaps the very one we were waiting to hear.

Another personal benefit is an increase in our own energy level. As we send love energy to others, we become the channel for an energy that originates with the divine source and moves through us, like a cup filling and spilling over to others. Often one of the fastest ways of regaining our inner divine connection when we feel separated is to uplift someone else.

UPLIFTING OTHERS IN GROUPS

The process of uplifting others leaps to new heights when we practice it in a group setting. Imagine what happens when members of a group are all interacting in this intentional manner. Each person focuses on the best self, the genius, the light in the faces of all the others, and they all simultaneously reciprocate.

Once again, implementing this procedure is a matter of intent, beginning as soon as the group starts its interaction. As the first person begins to speak, everyone else searches for and finds the higher-self expression on his or her face and begins to focus there, sending love and energy. The result is that the person feels a flow of energy coming from the other members of the group and achieves a higher sense of well-being and clarity. This leads to a greenhouse effect within the group, since the speaker who is being given energy adds the energy to his or her own and sends the accumulation back to the others, who experience an even higher energy to send back. In this way, the energy of the group compounds in an ever-increasing cycle of amplification.

This systematic increase in everyone's energy is the higher potential of every human group. It is the phenomenon referred to in the biblical passage "where two or more are gathered together in my name, there am I in the midst of them." Connecting with and amplifying the amount of divine energy is the true purpose of coming together in groups. Regardless of whether the group is part of a church or a technical work team, this process can enhance the creative power of the individuals involved to incredibly high levels.

IDEAL GROUP PROCESS

Let's imagine that everyone in an ideal group understands the potential energy levels that can be attained. Once assembled, each person would make sure that he or she is centered and connected inwardly with divine love and energy. Additionally, each would be aware of his or her overall life truth and current questions and live in a state of ready anticipation, awaiting synchronicity.

At the point that someone begins to speak, the members would intentionally focus on the highest-self expression that they can detect on the speaker's face. In this way, they know themselves to be intentionally sending love and energy to uplift this person. When the first speaker is done, the energy will shift naturally to another person. When this shift occurs, most members of the group will feel a lull in the energy. But the person who is supposed to speak next will feel a rush of inspiration as an idea, a truth, enters his or her mind.

Each of us, of course, has had this experience many times. We suddenly have something to say, and if the group is in tune, it will give us space to make our contribution. In our ideal group, the other members will feel who is supposed to speak next and simultaneously shift their focus to this individual.

COMMON PROBLEMS IN GROUPS

This transition from speaker to speaker can be tricky because more than one person may want to speak at the same time. When this happens, I believe one of the speakers is out of phase, perhaps not listening closely and trying to interject an idea he had thought of earlier. When an untimely idea is forced into the discussion, the group experiences a mild letdown in energy and senses that the new speaker inappropriately changed the subject. Always, there is a most appropriate speaker, someone who has the perfect idea that will expand the topic being discussed and move it in an insightful direction.

Grandstanding

Other problems can sidetrack group functioning as well. Grandstanding occurs when a member who is speaking keeps the floor longer than is appropriate. It usually occurs in the following manner: The group is flowing nicely. Each member carries the intention to send as much energy to everyone else as possible. Then, as the energy naturally begins to shift to someone else, the speaker fails to notice and continues with his own ideas, thinking of other things to say in spite of the group's decreasing attention.

The other members have the perception that the group is now out of its best flow and usually become restless. In extreme cases, the group might degenerate into a battle of egos as the confusion leads several members to vie for the floor, each thinking that he or she has something better to say.

Grandstanding usually reflects a problem with inner security. As the person is speaking, he is naturally filled with energy and uplifted. If this is a state the person cannot approximate when alone, he will hesitate to let go just because the energy of the group feels so good. The person hangs on, hoping to keep the attention and energy of the others as long as possible. This kind of insecurity is common and just means that the person should go back to work on strengthening inner energy and practice giving energy rather than receiving it.

The key to overcoming the problem of grandstanding is immediate recognition. If everyone sees what is occurring, the problem can be averted with as little disruption to the group as possible. The ideal solution, of course, is for the speaker to see what is taking place and stop himself. If that doesn't happen, the person who felt the energy move to him or her can intervene diplomatically by saying something such as, "Can we return to the point you made earlier? I'd like to comment." If the current speaker doesn't allow this, other members can intervene as well, moving the energy finally to the correct person.

Blocking

Another problem that often disrupts a group is blocking. Blocking is also the result of insecurity on the part of someone who attempts to gain energy and attention by always taking a contrary position. There are many reasons that such insecurity can arise in a group, but often the catalyst is a comment one of the members makes about a particular topic, or it may be some aspect of another member's personality that triggers a reaction.[3]

Blocking can be recognized because as the group is going forward, one member interrupts, taking exception with what the speaker is saying. Sometimes speakers will disagree naturally as a result of the true energy flow, in which case others will shift their attention to the new speaker's point. However, blocking occurs when a member speaks even though the energy has not shifted, and the general feeling on the part of the group is that the blocker has interrupted.

Another sign of this problem is that when other group members speak in support of the first speaker, the blocker continues to argue, often repeating his points. Usually, a person who blocks once continues to interrupt in a similar fashion over and over, creating a regular pattern of bids for attention. Blocking is a very serious problem in a group because it can effectively thwart all forward movement.

Like the grandstander, the blocker must be confronted diplomatically. If the blocking is general, anyone can intervene. But if the blocking is focused on a particular individual, the person targeted may be in the best position to confront the blocker, at least at first.

As with confronting a control drama, the situation must be brought into awareness. I would recommend that the confrontation be done in private, outside the group. Only if this doesn't work should the problem be discussed publicly. If the members are of high enough awareness, the issue can be spoken of effectively without any overreactions or blaming.

Acquiescing

Another problem that can befall groups occurs when the energy of the group moves to a particular member who fails to take her turn to speak. Once again, this would feel like a letdown of energy, a lull in the flow. The group might have been engaged in a perfect conversation, proceeding for a long period of time, when as usual, the energy of the current speaker begins to wane and shift to someone else—only the new person is silent. The members look at one another in confusion, or perhaps someone actually picks up on the person who should be speaking and looks her way, but still nothing happens. The person remains quiet.

Most of us probably know what it feels like to acquiesce. At some point, we have been participating in a group, listening intently, when we feel a burst of energy as we receive an idea, an insight or point of clarity for the topic at hand. There is a pause as the energy shifts our way, but instead of speaking up, we hesitate.

When this occurs, it prevents the group from being as effective as it could be. The contribution of every member at the right time is critical to the overall flow of truth. Often the eventual outcome, in terms of productivity, can be severely limited by just one person who acquiesces. The basis of this problem, of course, lies in the person's self-confidence and trust level with the other members of the group. Sometimes acquiescence can be prevented or kept to a minimum just by making sure the members are comfortable with each other, or by merely slowing the group process down.

When many members are inspired, the pace of discussion can accelerate too fast, so that not enough time is allowed for each speaker. If this pace is consciously slowed, the more timid members, who aren't as accustomed to the group process, have time to act.

We've all been the grandstander, blocker, or acquiescer at one time or another. But, by being conscious of these pitfalls in group dynamics, we can also all learn to avoid these problems. Any glitch in the group dynamic can be effectively overcome if the group's members stay alert and openly discuss any difficulties they perceive.

SUPPORT GROUPS

Many people are already meeting with others in organized support groups.[4] There are many spiritual benefits to this kind of group process. Support groups range from those oriented around addiction issues (which focus on certain defined problems such as alcoholism, drugs, codependency, overeating, or shopping) to groups involving particular life issues (such as parenting, living alone, dealing with death and dying, separating, divorcing, or finding the right job).

There is also a more general type of support group that is pursuing more positive and proactive issues. This kind of group focuses on expanding creative and intuitive power and synchronistic experience. Such groups give the members a forum in which to reality-test their spiritual perceptions and dreams. The goal of such groups is to keep every member's energy level high so that they can help one another continue growing by amplifying their energy and perception together.

HEALING AND HEALTH

Many of these groups pay special attention to each member's health needs. They might even place each member in the center of the group and project energy and healing intention toward him or her, visualizing the atoms of the person's body vibrating in perfect order. As has been scientifically demonstrated, this kind of focused group intention can work as a force of prayer that makes a difference.

If you are a member of a support group already, I recommend that this procedure be incorporated into your discussion on a regular basis. Simply make a circle with the group and alternate positions inside the circle as you beam healthful intentions toward one another. Certainly, such a practice should never be substituted for consulting a health care professional when appropriate, but we know that this process works to sustain the energy of health.

FINDING A GROUP

If you're not currently in a group, you may reach a time in your life when your current question becomes "How can I find a group?" At that point, stay alert and synchronicity should place the right group in your path. Remember, however, that working to keep your inner energy level high will help optimize group functioning, because if we come to a group feeling insecure, we will look to the group as a primary source of energy. When this occurs, we become more interested in receiving than giving, and the other members will experience this dependence as a drain on their energy.

Becoming aware of our control drama and discovering our general truth are steps that can be expedited when pursued within a group context, provided the whole group is devoted to the task. Group dialogue is also beneficial when we are examining our current life question, exploring intuitions, interpreting dreams, and discerning the meaning of a particular synchronicity.

Once we are ready and can maintain the energy, I believe our best group will present itself. Occasionally, however, I have seen a person who seems ready but still can't find a group. I've always believed that if you are ready for a group and can't find one, then you are meant to start one. That might sound difficult, but I believe all we have to do is declare ourselves a group and stay alert. Soon we will find ourselves in the grocery store or at the mall talking to someone who will casually mention that she is looking for a group, too. Suddenly, one has formed.

ROMANCE

As we consider our new interpersonal ethic, no issue is more pressing than how to pursue romantic relationships. In light of the new spiritual awareness, we seem to be asking again the age-old questions: How do we make our romantic relationships last? Why does romantic love often end, degenerating into a complex power struggle?

The usual romantic experience begins easily enough. We look around and wham! There before us is the person of our dreams. The first conversation confirms it. Unlike the one-sided attractions we've all experienced, this one seems to be real; the feeling is mutual. We find countless values and lifestyle preferences in common.

And oh, the emotion! The love bubbles forth and the sex is steamy and soulful. Perhaps over time, we date each other exclusively or marry, making plans far into the future. For perhaps the first time in many years, we feel content, and even comment that we have found the missing piece of ourselves, the person that makes life worth living.

And then something happens. One day we look over and notice something not quite right about the situation. Our partner has a behavior that doesn't seem to live up to the spirit of the romance. He or she isn't giving us the attention we felt when the relationship began. Or perhaps we realize that in our overexuberance, we failed to notice that in some area of the relationship the person never gave us the attention we really needed. Amazingly, at the same time, we realize that our partner has his or her own set of complaints about us, finding fault with who we are and the way we act. We begin to defend ourselves, as does our partner, and the typical power struggle officially begins.

STRUGGLING FOR THE ENERGY

From the perspective of the new spiritual awareness, we now know what happens. Love ends and evolves into a power struggle because we begin to depend on energy from each other, rather than from our own inner connection with the divine.

Let's look at the social dynamic of how this problem usually manifests. According to the old materialistic worldview, a little boy grows up with a mother who cares, who nurtures him and monitors his safety. The father is more demanding: after all, the son must learn the hard truth of the world to become a man. In the child's mind, the mother becomes a magical figure. She may have to be kept at arm's length if the nurturing is too smothering, but he expects her to be there, in a psychological sense, whenever his energy level is down.

A little girl is also first nurtured by the mother. But for her, the mother is also the one who is demanding, because she feels most responsible to teach the little girl the role of a woman. The father, at least in the early formative years, can be the magical figure who dotes on her and places her on a pedestal. He is always there in her fantasies to make her feel safe.

This stereotypical division of roles and perceived attitudes affects us still. We may claim that in the modern world these role divisions have no meaning, but unconscious psychological programming often raises its head in relationships and becomes the basis for energy power struggles. Couples begin to find fault and be dissatisfied with each other because they need more from the other person than can ever be given.

When we first come together in love, we join our energies in a way that gives us the feeling of completeness. Our partner provides not just the memory of our nurturing parent but the feel of that relationship as well. Our fantasies project on our all-too-human partner the magical illusion we first experienced with our fathers or mothers as children. Thus, we often never see the depth of who our partner really is: we see only what we fantasize.

As the relationship progresses, that "in love" feeling begins to wane for both partners, as each falls short of the magical image the other has projected on him or her. The male makes financial mistakes or loses his job or is late because he went to a ball game. The female isn't there to nurture when things aren't going well. The bubble of perfection begins to collapse.

In some cases, the disappointment with our partners is so great that we immediately make plans to leave the relationship, to find another dream lover who won't let us down. In such cases, we just begin the cycle all over again. In other cases, the lovers stay together but are locked in a repetitive pattern of control dramas.

Yet now, because of our expanding awareness, we have other options. We can instead choose to act based on the energy dynamics that underlie the difficulty.

INTEGRATING THE INNER
MALE AND FEMALE

Until now we have spoken of transcendent or mystical experiences as the way to open up our connection with divine energy in the form of a single surge of energy that we experience as love, lightness, and security—and so it is. But as we experience this energy, it also has male and female characteristics. As Carl Jung and other noted psychologists have shown in their studies of the archetypal nature of our psyche, if we are to open up to the full potential of transpersonal awareness, we must become conscious of and integrate both the female and male aspects of our higher selves.[5]

If we are male, in order to connect with the divine energy within, we must locate, court, and finally engage the energy of the female nurturer within our own being. If we are female, we must find the male provider and protector and risk-taker inside ourselves.

With this truth in mind, we see the male/female power struggle for what it is: symptoms of a vast problem our society has loosely called codependence.[6] When two people come together and fall in love, they are really merging their energy fields in a way that provides the missing part of themselves—male or female. They begin to depend on that energy. As the relationship progresses, however, each begins to doubt the other and the energy levels collapse. Then both partners fall back into their respective control dramas, trying to regain the energy.

If we are to achieve lasting relationships rather than truces in the cold war, we must understand the energy dynamics involved before engaging in a romance. We all must find the opposite sexual energy within ourselves before we make ourselves available for a lasting relationship. In a sense, attaining this balance of the male and female within each of us must become as big a part of the adolescent rite of passage as graduating from high school or learning to drive. None of us can have a higher-quality relationship until we become spiritually secure and complete inside.

BEING OKAY ALONE

How do we know whether we have achieved this male/female balance of energy and moved toward inner security? I believe one measure is the ability to feel secure and productive while living alone. This means without roommates or other people with whom we attach ourselves every waking moment. We must be okay making our own meals and eating them not in huge spoonfuls in front of the stove, but elegantly, by candlelight, at a fully set table by ourselves. Periodically, we must be comfortable with taking ourselves out on a date—to a movie, perhaps—or wining and dining ourselves as we would another loved one.

Similarly, we must care for ourselves financially, plan

for the future, negotiate our own deals, and develop our own leisure activities. The person we must rely on to be whole is the divine we find within ourselves, and this doesn't imply selfishness or a detached withdrawal from the rest of society. In fact, I would argue that we can be involved with the rest of society in a healthy way only when we integrate our full energy within.

Only then do we face the possibility of true romantic relationships. As the respected couples' therapist Harville Hendrix points out in his groundbreaking books *Getting the Love You Want* and *Keeping the Love You Find*,[7] as long as we are looking for our energy to come to us from another, we will be trapped in relationships that are no more than arenas for power struggles.

I believe that the partnerships through which we play out and finally become aware of our problems of power struggles come to us synchronistically and are in fact holy relationships just as *A Course in Miracles* attests.[8] The picture of our addictions comes to us over and over again in the form of different people until we get the message. These relationships occur so we can transcend our need for them, as unromantic as that sounds; only then can we come back to our reliance on inner divine connection for love and security. If we are single, person after person will approach us for a codependent match. If we jump from one to another, nothing will be gained. Only by resisting the coupling can we hold out for time to strengthen our inner connection and gain the energy to find our more fitting soulmate.

CURRENT RELATIONSHIPS

Given these concerns, what are we to do with our current relationships?

I believe that the challenge of integrating our two gender energies can be addressed while remaining in a relationship—but only if both people understand the energy dynamics of the process and work on it together. Attempting the process alone is much more difficult.

The answer is for each couple to come back to love when power struggles erupt. Be alert to what is occurring when a fight begins. One or both partners are dissatisfied with the other's behavior because it fails to measure up to the memory of the ideal or magical parent they project on each other and because their inner source of energy is weak. We need the person to live up to this ideal because this allows us in our own minds to relax and count on our partner for our security. This projection, and indeed, the whole attempt to rely on another as a substitute for inner divine energy, never works, and it always breaks down into the power struggle again.

The solution is to come back to a state of love, and of inner security, even while the battle is progressing, and to uplift the other person with all your might. To do this, you need to have experienced some kind of mystical, transcendent connection in the past, which you can now remember and go back to. In other words, coming back to love is not an idea; it is a real transformative moment, in which we reach back for a state of love and security that stems from divine energy within.

Again, whether or not we are truly doing this is always an individual assessment. *A Course in Miracles* would hold that two people together can reach that state right in the middle of a fight if they go deeply enough into love. Yet, in the heat of a power struggle, it is very difficult to do so. For many people who find themselves in a troubled partnership, a physical separation is in order—at least a separation in time spent together. This would only work, however, if both people take this time to find the mystical opening, the possibility of transcendent experience for themselves, and then bring that capability back to the relationship.

What, though, do we do if we feel in our hearts that we are just in the wrong relationship? Do we abandon the partnership? This is an option many people choose, but unless we hold out for personal wholeness before we engage in another romantic relationship, we'll just repeat the patterns of our old partnerships again and again.

How do we know when we are ready, when we have succeeded in balancing the male and female within ourselves? There are therapists who maintain that no matter how clear we think we are, no matter how much energy we have reached alone, our powers of inner love and security will still be tested in our relationships, and I'm sure this is true. But I'm also convinced that the energy and security we learn to tap internally is the most important factor in success.

PARENTING

No human activity is illuminated by the emerging spiritual awareness more than parenting, and in no area of life is it more important to apply the new interpersonal ethic. As our spiritual awareness expands, our responsibility to our children increases and becomes more clear. Just as we came to our parents to learn the world, our children have chosen us. They want to learn our way of being, how we determine the appropriate reaction to various situations, and our strategy of expectation that helps create the future. And, as we shall see in the coming chapters, this relationship between the generations is the long-term mechanism for human evolution and progress itself. What human society can ultimately achieve depends, to a large extent, on how consciously each of us can engage in this process.

The key is to remember where we are as our personal awareness expands and to communicate the full scope of that awareness to our children. It is easy to regress to the old materialistic worldview we learned from our own parents, telling ourselves that a child cannot grasp the complications of the inner growth we are experiencing. Too often, we focus instead on the material and social side of life—raising our children more or less the way we were raised.

Finding the simple words for communicating our dreams and spiritual experience is the most important part of parenting. There are ways to express our beliefs about divine energy within, how control dramas get in the way, and the guiding force of synchronicity that a child will understand, if only we find the courage to try.

STAYING CENTERED WHEN DISCIPLINING

Another important aspect of parenting emphasized by the new ethic is the act of discipline. We now have a good scientific understanding of what goes wrong in many families, and society is outraged at the extent of outright abuse that has occurred in the past. Once, we hid our eyes from the degree of incest and violence that existed in our families, but no longer. Now we watch like hawks for signs of poor parenting.

But when we look at parenting from the point of view of energy dynamics, we see that we must also guard against the more subtle forms of abuse: draining our children's energy just by the way we interact. In a sense, we must learn to walk a narrow road. If we have learned anything in the last two generations, it is that we can also hurt children by taking a totally hands-off approach to discipline. Children must be stopped when they are mistreating others or ignoring the realities of the world. The parent must teach children with a kind of tough love. Learning how to live with others—becoming socialized—is what our children come to us for, and to fail in these lessons is to let them down. We must find a way to teach our children consequences without oppressing them in the process.

This balanced approach begins, I believe, with a constant check of our own energy level. In each interaction with our children, we must assess whether we have remained in connection with our inner energy and so are able to hold an intention of love, regardless of the situation. The worst thing that can occur is for us to go unconscious, fall into our old control drama, and, for example, go into an Interrogator mode with our children, hovering about them and thus pulling their energy into us. All this will do is force them to design a control drama of their own as a means of defense.

Our challenge is to remember the underlying energy dynamics. When our children are ignoring rules and rushing forward without consciousness, we can stop and correct them at the same time we are uplifting them, focusing on the genius in their faces. What we want to do is convey the psychological message: What you did was inappropriate, but you are good.

Our goal is to always be there with our energy, teaching them our view of the world and our truth of what they must consider in order to have a full life—including the expectation that they eventually find their own connection with the divine. This is the point at which we must be prepared to let them go in their own direction.

WHY DID OUR CHILDREN CHOOSE US?

Why did our children choose us? If in some higher-self sense we chose our own parents, and the experiences with them have led to a general preparation that helped awaken us to a truth to tell the world, we know that the same process is happening with our own children. By modeling who we really are, we are giving them a preparation that they came to us to receive.

We must be careful, however, in trying to figure out what the preparation is or what their truths should be, because no one is qualified to evaluate that experience but them, sometime in the future. It is a great mistake as parents, in my opinion, to assume we know for sure what our children are supposed to do and be. Such presumption only leads to a narrowing of options for these souls in our care, a mistake that can create decades of resentment.

That is not to say that we don't have intuitions about the meaning of our children's lives. I think we do. What parent doesn't find herself daydreaming about her children's futures, only to sense that unmistakable feeling that what she saw was a real possibility? Parents can have special insights into not only educational and career plans but various psychological challenges that our children must become aware of if their lives are to fulfill their own destinies.

So perhaps what should be said is that while we will experience intuitive visions about our children's future paths, we must not in any sense jump to conclusions or create self-fulfilling prophecies. To do so takes away our children's agency over their own futures, which will always be more broad and synchronistic than our intuitions. All we can do is gently share our feelings while resisting the temptation to look over their shoulders constantly or to steer them around every dead end. The mistakes they make on their own often provide important lessons that will prove essential to them later in life.

THE LARGER PICTURE OF PARENTING

I believe that in order to fully grasp the spiritual implications of parenting, we must view this area of life from the broadest perspective. Our children are here with us because they want to learn our view of what life is about, including our spiritual beliefs. To repeat, nothing is more important than sharing our lives with our children openly. Certainly, we must be conscious of age appropriateness when discussing certain issues, but we must also be honest. We can find ways to communicate what we are going through, what we have discovered spiritually about getting the most from life, that our children can hear and understand.

Another problem can occur in families when a mother or father makes a career out of the act of parenting itself. I don't mean the full-time housewife or househusband, who presumably continues to grow and evolve. I am referring to those who stop living themselves and begin to focus all their attention on their children and live vicariously through their children's experiences, both successful and unsuccessful.

Even worse is the parent who sets the child up as the determinant of his or her self-esteem and social status, as we see in parents who overly invest in Little League successes and child beauty contests. Of utmost importance is to continue to be creative and to evolve our truth in our own right. Our children are born to us so they can see our lives in action, and in doing so, be able to learn from this growth and to build upon it.

In the end, of course, it is a two-way street. Our children help us clarify our own meaning and synchronistic growth. If we are the givers of energy at first, very soon our children begin to give back to us important synchronistic messages. As they emulate our behavior, they show us ourselves in a clearer way. And this includes more than our verbal expressions and way of talking. Later it includes our very attitudes and way of creating.

If we refuse to deal with certain dramas and negative reactions, these will also come back to us reflected in the behavior of our children. In this way, as we shall see later, the sins of the father are visited on the children in a sociologically real way. If nothing else, this fact should motivate us even more to stay clear and connected with inner energy and to model a life that is consciously evolving.

LIVING THE NEW ETHIC

As we have seen, the scope of the new interpersonal ethic is very large. Once we reach the level of awareness in which we know that most of our synchronicity arrives through other people, we begin to use the energy dynamics we've learned to uplift all the people in our lives. As we've seen, this works both individually and in groups of all kinds, and is especially important in romantic relationships. Romance challenges our ability to stay centered and connected and reinforces the need to rely on our own inner source of divine energy for security. Always, the ethic is to give energy to our partners, not take, and this ability determines how great the relationship can turn out to be.

With children, once again, the ethic is to give energy,

to honestly guide without overcontrolling, and to let them learn who we really are. The payoff is the same rich synchronicity that comes back to us when we exercise this ethic with everyone. The more love and energy we give, the more rapidly the synchronistic messages come to us, and the more creative, effective, and inspiring will be our individual lives.

Yet I believe an even deeper motivation lies at the heart of adopting this new ethic. Deep inside we know that as a critical number of individuals maintain their energy at a certain level and strive to live this ethic, the world is preparing to take great leaps in evolution.

10

MOVING TOWARD A SPIRITUAL CULTURE

Our next step in living the new spiritual awareness begins with a shared intuition of where our evolution in consciousness is leading. What would be happening, for instance, if everyone were living the new awareness as we have described it so far? How would human culture change?

Pursuing the answers to these questions begins to open us up to an inner vision of human destiny, and I believe we can already see aspects of our culture in transformation.

THE IMPORTANCE OF TITHING

Ubiquitous among the classic mystical literature is the assertion that there exists a universal law of giving and receiving. Whether it is the biblical concept of "reaping what we sow" or the law of karma in the East, religions teach that our intentions and actions return to us, for better or worse. "What comes around goes around" is the contemporary way of expressing this idea.

Many religious and mystical thinkers have applied this principle to the ideal flow of money in society, relating this esoteric idea of cause and effect to the scriptural idea of *tithing*. Charles Fillmore, founder of Unity Church, Napoleon Hill, and Norman Vincent Peale all made the case that giving of our love and energy, including the giving of money, always creates an effect in the world that brings even more money and opportunity back our way.[1] As far as I'm aware, no one has done any formal research on this matter, but the anecdotal evidence in support of this principle, as more people try the process for themselves, seems to be mounting rapidly.

One problem in the past has been that traditional churches, influenced by the old paradigm that removed the mystery and miracle from the universe, spoke of tithings only during their yearly fund-raising. That made people feel tithing was just a way to support churches. However, I believe that our open sharing of spiritual experience in recent decades is quickly broadening our understanding of the tithing process. The belief seems to be growing that the act of giving engages a metaphysical process totally congruent with our knowledge that the universe is responsive.

Another issue in the past has been where to give our tithes. Some people still believe that only founded churches qualify, because they are the keepers of the faith and provide a constant stream of spiritual information. Others say that any gift of charity is essentially a tithe and thus engages the universe for a response. I think what we are discovering is that tithing is a process that must always be integrated into the rest of the synchronistic movement in our lives. In other words, we will know where to give based on the synchronicity of the situation.

From that view, tithes are of two kinds. One is intuitive, a response to an urge to give money to an individual or organization because we feel inwardly directed to do so. A friend of mine says he is guided by this question: If God couldn't come and sent you instead, what difference would God have made in the situation? At the highest level, we give because we are there. If we don't respond to the situation, who will?

The other kind of tithe, and the one that is especially significant for the transformation of human society, is the tithe that is given to our sources of spiritual information—that is to say, to the specific sources of our everyday synchronistic moments. Because churches and spiritual organizations can bring us information at just the right time, they will certainly continue to be the beneficiaries of tithes, but so will individuals. As we've seen, it is almost always the messages coming from other people that lead us forward in our journey. Tithing is a way to respond.

Let's imagine for a moment that everyone who is living his or her synchronistic growth begins to tithe others in this manner. A whole new type of economic flow would begin. We would give money spontaneously to the people who bring us messages, and, as we told our truth to others, money would come to us in exactly the same way. (On a personal note, I've received many tithes, and my policy is to pass on the money with a tithe of my own. And I would ask anyone who might want to tithe me in the future to please forward that money to a local charity.)

I believe spontaneous giving is supplementing our economic system, confirming the idea and the faith that synchronicity can supplement and extend the sole focus on logical planning held by the old paradigm. We are not giving up the large networks of people we already do business with in the usual economic way. We are spontaneously adding to them, freeing the whole global economic system to jump to a higher level of productivity.

THE NEW ECONOMY

Introducing the practice of synchronistically tithing also helps us adapt to several other economic trends that are disturbing: the downsizing of industries, businesses, and corporations and the stagnation of wages in the developed countries because of global competition.

Downsizing is not possible unless the remaining employees can increase their productivity, which is exactly what computers and improved communication systems allow. Increased wage competition is to be expected if the rest of the world is going to participate in the level of creativity we in the developed nations have achieved, so this trend will continue and we must adapt. This certainly doesn't mean that we should encourage developing countries to make the same mistakes that we have made, such as the wasteful use of resources or the exploitation of workers, but most of us would agree, I think, that they have a right to participate in the world economy.

So how do we deal with these issues? First of all, we have to see the larger picture of economic evolution.[2] In the United States, some of the most watched economic indicators are those measuring productivity, the amount of goods and services produced per unit of labor. If our production goes up, we think our economy is healthy and growing. Yet we must ask the question, where will this process end? Every year fewer and fewer people will provide ever more of the basic necessities of life.

Our challenge is to think of this evolution not as negative, but as extremely positive, because out of this process will ultimately come the liberation of our creative attention. We can see, I believe, that much of what we are going through is part of the destined economic evolution of the world, and we can orient ourselves best by becoming conscious of the process.

In the short run, we have to adapt to the shift from industrial manufacturing, which will become ever more automated, to jobs and businesses providing not goods, but information. And the data show that we already are. In the United States, increasingly more people are going into business for themselves—yet these businesses are not chiefly retail or storefront businesses requiring high amounts of capital; they are niche jobs, run out of individuals' homes. In America, nearly 35 million households now have a flexible home business, and most of these jobs are in the information sector.[3]

But I believe we can see in the long run that eventually our basic necessities will be totally automated and that our economic life will orient almost completely around the flow of timely information. At first, this will be information concerning the automation process, but eventually it will reflect our evolution into a spiritual culture and will involve information of a purely spiritual nature.

The implementation of tithing into the system will obviously facilitate this process, at first supplementing our incomes as the economy shifts, and then gradually replacing the old system of charging for our services with a system whereby one tells one's truth in an ongoing flow of synchronistic encounters and receives money as the recipients give tithes. As outrageous as this sounds from the point of view of the old competitive paradigm, I believe we can see that such a system is inherent in the operation of capitalism.

As we shall discuss later, if we are truly motivated by the capitalist principle of finding a need and filling it, this is the only possible future for our economy. The first stage in setting up such a system would be a basic right to ownership, through stock perhaps, of the automated industries. This would guarantee access to the needs of subsistence, after which we would earn income by providing synchronistic information and services. Eventually, under such a system, we could stop using currency altogether, just as science fiction writers have prophesied. This assumes, certainly, that the new spiritual awareness as we've pictured it so far has become a human reality.

In addition, key technological discoveries would have to take place, including a low-cost source of energy. But we are closer to these discoveries than ever before. According to Dr. Eugene F. Mallove, we are on the verge of making practical several new energy sources, including the much debated process of cold fusion.[4] If a lower-cost energy can be integrated into the world economy, automation will soar.

Most important of all, perhaps, is that we must begin

now to live this new economic idea. Will there be economic problems along the way? If William Greider is right in his recent book *One World, Ready or Not,*[5] we must be prepared for some economic disruption resulting from current financial speculating. According to Greider, the whole world is in the same position the United States faced in 1929: borrowing too much for the purpose of economic speculation. When the bubble burst in 1929, there was suddenly a general shortage of cash. Banks that had lent depositors' money for speculation failed and had to close their doors, and many lost their life savings.

In response, the United States implemented limits on domestic borrowing and instituted deposit insurance, and many other governments did the same. But in recent years, in response to the growing world market, governments have allowed financial capital to cross borders without much regulation, so that now there is a growing amount of money that is invested and speculated internationally in exactly the same ways that created economic failure in 1929. Today, this worldwide speculation crosses all the major currencies, without any one government being able to do much about it. Huge amounts of money can be borrowed in one country and invested speculatively in another with few limits. Could there be a misstep, a meltdown, that could seriously jeopardize the health of one or more countries' banking system or currency? Of course there could.

Such global problems only emphasize the need for

local economies to become stronger. Synchronistic tithing can ground and circumvent problems resulting from other excesses.

SYNCHRONICITY AND ENERGY

What about the other shifts in human culture that are resulting from the new spiritual awareness? Perhaps most important is the continued expansion of our personal energy levels. Once we experience the full inflow of energy during a mystical experience and the synchronicity of our lives begins to reveal our personal truth, we can systematically institute in our lives—as we deliver this truth—ever higher degrees of this original mystical energy. In other words, as we stay on the synchronistic path, we are able to live at ever higher states of energy.

And is this not the process that has been behind human history and striving from the very beginning? Ever since records have been kept, humans have grown stronger and lived longer with each successive generation. Further, human civilization has created ever more sophisticated examples of what we have always called genius. A greater percentage of the world's population than ever before in human history now lives an inspired and energetic life. In the past, we have explained this progress in terms of secular materialism—that is, in terms of better food, better hygiene, and advances in medicine.

Yet, as we have seen, the old materialistic worldview is itself evolving into a new understanding in which we know that in reality there is no material. At the most minute levels, the atoms of our bodies fade away into mere patterns of energy, vibratory waves that can shift form and reconstitute themselves in amazing ways. How else can we explain events such as spontaneous healing in which tumors disappear or tissues regenerate virtually overnight?[6] The progress of the generations is a progress of inspiration, faith, and confidence, and ever-increasing levels of inner energy.

THE LESSON OF SPORTS

If you speak with sports and exercise enthusiasts of all persuasions, you will find that most engage in the activity not because of the thrill of winning or to improve their appearance, but because of the inner rewards they feel. Running and other aerobic exercises bring on the thrill and euphoria of overcoming "the wall," that feeling that one can go no further. And once the strenuous activity is over, participants report that they feel lighter, calmer, more coordinated, able to move more easily.

We engage in sports and aerobic exercises because during and afterward we sense we are stronger, more energized, even smarter. And every year, we get better at it for a longer period of time. Bodybuilding, running, martial arts, tennis, ice-skating, jumping, golf, swimming, gymnastics—each has a performance envelope that is constantly being pushed outward as old records give way to new excellence.

The old worldview that reduces our bodies to muscles, bones, and ligaments has no real explanation for where this process will end. If pressed, a materialist will say that the human body will ultimately reach its full potential, so that a runner can then run no faster, or a weight lifter can raise not another pound, or a tennis player can surely not reach that ball blistered crosscourt. Yet, like the four-minute mile, every so-called barrier will be crossed. We continue to move faster with better coordination and timing and lightness.

So where will it end? The only answer that meets the facts is that it won't end. Sooner or later, those athletes running the 100-meter dash will be moving so fast that their bodies will instantly change form to respond to the will's certainty of what can be achieved. As they move down the track, they will be mere streaks of light.

THE TESTIMONY OF THE YOGIS

Throughout history, the East has produced men who have likewise pushed the envelope of human ability. In his important work *The Future of the Body*, author Michael Murphy brought together an astounding collection of documented cases of unusual bodily transformation, including the ability to levitate, spontaneous changes in form, and the performance of unbelievable feats of strength.[7] Many thinkers in the Eastern tradition consider these attributes the optimal result of yogic practice, still rare perhaps, but the expected outcome of years of meditation and movement practice.

For centuries, the West has been completely astounded by such ability. The Bible tells us that Jesus was seen to appear and disappear at will, walk on water, and so forth, but after Newton formalized the vision of a clockwork universe, such abilities were seen as magical or metaphoric, the stuff of myth or hoax, but certainly not an example of real human ability. Later, the Christian church explained these abilities as the mark of a deity, and certainly nothing that humans could possibly emulate.

Yet as Michael Murphy has shown, examples of transcendent ability abound in both Western and Eastern history, and the awakening happening today includes a revision of what is possible not just for special adepts but for you and me as well.

WHERE WE ARE GOING

As we ponder these developments, we are envisioning how human culture will change in the future. And this vision will give us further courage to shift our lifestyles and fully embrace the spiritual world in which we live.

The new world, as we have seen, can be one of great creativity and personal fulfillment. Imagine how life will be once most of the people we find ourselves talking with know the process and expect each conversation to be special and carry a message.

The pace and style of human interaction will completely change, and this will quickly begin to impact the economy. Once enough of us understand and experientially prove that the principle of tithing works, we will embrace this process fully, synchronistically giving a percentage of our income to the sources we feel urged to support. In the same way, opportunity and finances will come right back to us, quite magically, congruent with our expectations. The evidence is in the outcome.

This giving economy will, as we discussed, first supplement our incomes as technological advances automate more and more of our material needs, and then will characterize the information age completely as our collective focus shifts from accumulating material security to engaging in the higher inspiration of synchronistic growth. And, once again, as the synchronicity continues and the inspiration soars, our bodies will be reaching ever higher levels of energy until we become spiritual beings of light.

11

THE VIEW FROM
THE AFTERLIFE

If our destiny is to become spiritual beings on earth, what about the rest of the story: the birth and death process itself? What will we discover about the heavenly dimension from which we come and to which we return when our time here is over?

According to the latest polls, a great majority of Americans believe in the Afterlife, and the percentage is even higher in many other countries around the world. Yet by all accounts, our current notions about the After-life are far different from the idea of heaven and hell predominant in the old materialistic culture.[1]

In the past, we envisioned the Afterlife as a cute caricature of angels and harps and clouds, because our psychological stance of denying the mystery posed by death kept us from contemplating the subject in any detail. To look any closer meant we had to squarely face our own death as a real event, and that was something for which human culture, at least in the West, had no time.

But, as we saw, the humanistic psychology of the mid-twentieth century began to erode our denial. Now we are gaining the ability not only to face death as a natural part of life but to pursue the details of what seems to happen during this process. Over the last several decades, our culture has been flooded with new information. A constant stream of books about the near-death experience has appeared, providing firsthand reports from individuals who have been clinically dead for a period of time and then have come back to life. Most of them returned because they felt, or were told, that they had something left to do.

In addition, several well-respected researchers such as Kenneth Ring and Melvin Morse have scientifically investigated near-death experiences, providing widely dispersed and credible summaries for the general public.[2]

Movies have further disseminated this information about the Afterlife and made it seem more real. Who, for instance, wasn't totally suspended in the realism of the movie *Always,* a love story about a Forest Service flier who saved the life of a friend but lost his own in a fiery airplane explosion? He later found himself walking on the ground, thinking he must have somehow avoided death. It took the counsel of a guiding spirit to convince him that he indeed did die, and that he himself must now act as a guiding spirit to a bumbling pilot sent to take his place. The realism of that relationship was awe-inspiring.

Another good example is the movie *Ghost,* a story of a man who was killed in a robbery attempt, yet found himself still on earth, able to see everything that was going on but unable to make his presence known to others. He remained to help protect a friend from the murderer, who was after a secret computer password. As the movie progressed, he met other ghosts, learned how they made contact with those still alive, and met a psychic who could actually hear him.

These movies present fascinating themes that reflect an emerging knowledge about what we can expect after death. Many questions still remain, but because of the dispersal of Afterlife information, we are beginning to form a clearer picture of death, and this knowledge is widening our perspective about our earthly existence and evolution.

THE NEAR-DEATH EXPERIENCE

One amazing aspect of the near-death experience is that most people who die and come back tell similar stories about what occurred. Many, for instance, leave their bodies and hover, at first, right above their beds or at the scene of an accident in which they were injured, often watching resuscitation attempts and overhearing precise conversations that are verified at a later date.

Some even hang around the hospital for a while before asking, "Now what?" That question usually brings on a feeling of movement and entry into what is always described as a tunnel of light. Others never look around at all after death; they immediately move into this tunnel.

The tunnel sometimes leads to a waiting or resting area of warm, white light, where the person is bathed in a feeling of immense love and peace. Often the person is met by deceased relatives and friends who explain his situation; usually, he feels as though he has returned home and resists returning to the earthly plane.

At some point, however, those undergoing a near-death experience have what is commonly referred to as a Life Review. Afterward they are sometimes given a choice as to whether they may stay or go back. At other times, they are told they definitely must go back and why. Almost always, those undergoing a near-death experience perceive, in a moment of clarity and vision, what they have left to do on earth.

To a person, their lives are changed dramatically by their near-death experience. Most pursue lives of inspiration, giving, and love.[3]

THE LIFE REVIEW

The Life Review is one of the most fascinating aspects of the near-death experience. Usually, individuals report envisioning their whole lives flashing before their eyes, not so much like a movie but as a holographic representation. They see everything in great detail and experience their lives being judged not by others, but by themselves. It is as if their consciousness has expanded and united with a larger divine intelligence.

From this place of higher understanding, individuals undergoing a near-death experience say that during the review process, they understand the improper decisions they made and how they could have handled specific situations better. The review is both intensely painful and overwhelmingly joyful, depending on what they are watching. When they review an incident where they emotionally hurt someone, they actually feel the pain that the person felt, as though they are inside the other's body.

Conversely, they are also able to see and feel the joy and love they engendered in others, by actually being them. Because of this intense depth of empathy, most people who have had a near-death experience return to life with a strong determination not to make the same mistakes again and to multiply the times they help others. Each comment to an individual, each interaction with a friend or a child, each thought sent out into the world about someone else, now takes on heightened meaning, for the person knows that each of these actions will one day be relived and reviewed.

It seems that at some level we have always known about the Life Review. Who hasn't heard, for instance, of someone, after a brush with death, remarking, "My whole life flashed before me"? Similarly, much of sacred literature and scripture devoted to judgment after death has pointed to a Life Review of some kind. Now, however, we are bringing the details of that experience into consciousness. We are judged when we die, but seemingly we are judged not by a vengeful God, but by a divine consciousness of which we are a part.

One result of this information becoming known is that we can all slow down and become more aware of the effect of our actions. It gives us an even greater understanding of why we should always consciously uplift others. We may still have lapses in judgment, but now we can stop ourselves periodically and review how we are doing, in effect experiencing a Life Review in our own minds, in advance. I believe we will find that this is the real process of repentance.

THE PROBLEM OF EVIL

What about the devil and the conspiracy of fallen angels of which so many religious traditions speak? None of the research on near-death experiences has found any evidence of such antics.

The near-death phenomenon confirms that there is only one divine force in the universe, and that force is positive. The problem of evil is all about human ego and fear, which alienate us from this creative force. When we humans are connected with this divinity, both here and in the Afterlife, our security comes from within. When we are alienated from the divine source, we look for security outside ourselves in some form of ego gratification and energy-stealing control dramas.

As we saw in Chapter 5, humans devise all manner of devices to narrow their experience and push away the anxiety of life. All evil, from the sordid fetishes of the molester to the desperate gambles of the white-collar criminal, is merely a way to repress the fear of lostness, if only for a moment. Evil and hell are internal states.

Most violent criminals grow up in a deprived environment characterized by neglect, outright abuse, and great fear. A child in such an environment is often beaten for crying, sometimes sexually tortured by parents and siblings, terrorized by older children in the neighborhood, and essentially abandoned to fend for himself. Under these circumstances, the amount of daily fear is inconceivable to those of us who grew up in more secure family situations. These children must find some way to cope, to push the terror and anxiety out of their minds.

A typical coping mechanism in this situation is some kind of fetish or obsession that can be repeated enough to create a sense of control. At superficial levels of anxiety, this activity can simply be the bravado of the mugger. At more extreme levels, it is the torturous activities of a serial killer or the dehumanization of a terrorist. All this behavior must be understood as a defense mechanism against the great fear that results from spiritual disconnection.[4]

THE NATURE OF HELL

The problem with constructing delusional devices to ward off anxiety is that they regularly break down. They relieve the symptom—anxiety—rather than the true illness of fear and insecurity, so in the long run they are doomed to failure. In the case of the mugger, expressing the tough-guy bravado and holding up tourists might work for a while, but sooner or later the horrors of childhood and the terror of lostness pour back into consciousness. Like the drug user who needs an increasingly larger fix to get the same results, the mugger must accelerate his activity, his macho and recklessness, in order to push his anxiety away again. Yet this action puts him in ever more dangerous situations, and his fear only increases.

This scenario can be played out, as well, by the white-collar criminal whose delusions finally catch up with him or by anyone whose use of drugs, working, shopping, eating, watching sports, or pursuing sex gets out of control. Whatever the crutch or obsessive behavior, it never addresses the root cause and is doomed to break down; the angst creeps back in and we are driven onward in our never-ending flight from disconnection. This is the nature of hell on earth—and according to much of the information coming in from near-death and out-of-body researchers, it is the nature of hell in the Afterlife as well.

Robert Monroe reported that during his travels in the Afterlife dimension he regularly saw hellishly delusional constructions devised by groups of souls who obsessively pursued sex as a defensive illusion against their lostness.[5] In Ruth Montgomery's automatic writing of Arthur Ford's descriptions of the Afterlife, she noted that certain souls could not wake up to heaven after death, caught up, no doubt, in the same illusions they devised in life.[6]

Such accounts suggest there is also great effort on the part of other beings in the Afterlife dimension to intervene with these deluded souls. They probably do so using the same process of uplifting that we already know about: the process of focusing on the soul's higher self and projecting energy until the soul wakes up, cuts through the obsessive activity, and begins to open up to the divine inside—which is the only real cure for any obsessive activity.

Throughout these reports, however, there is no sign of a malevolent conspiracy. I think we have to conclude that the fallen angels of Scripture are symbolic. As thinkers from Carl Jung to Joseph Campbell have suggested, the scriptural fall from grace, including the story of Satan's fall and his banishment to hell, are merely metaphors for the pitfalls inherent in human evolution. In its evolutionary journey toward spirituality, humanity has had to emerge from unconsciousness by developing ego strength and becoming self-aware. Yet, to progress further, our egos must take a backseat to the higher self and stop resisting the act of letting-go to the transcendent experience.

All of us have observed the rebellions of an adolescent who is trying to be someone and fashion a unique identity separate from that of his parents. In just this same way, in order to develop our independent ego, we have pulled away from our intuitive source and tried to run our lives totally by ourselves. One could even say that Western culture, as a whole, has been in this state of rebellion for four or five hundred years, having decided, because of the fear, to deny the larger aspect of our being.

In a sense, the symbolism of a devil out there, ready to foil our lives if we stray too far from God, is accurate, because the ego, detached from the divine within, is capable of exactly that.

THE BIRTH VISION

Another characteristic of the near-death experience that enhances our understanding of earthly life is the Birth Vision. This is an overall, panoramic image of our individual best-case life story, which some have reported seeing in advance of returning from a near-death experience.[7] When they receive the Birth Vision, individuals report they can see why they should come back, because they understand what they have left unfinished here on earth.

Knowing that this vision exists reinforces the idea that each of us can discover our true destiny, even though we have not had a near-death experience. We have already seen how an understanding of our past and all that has happened to us can help us sense the truth we are destined to tell the world. But also available to our consciousness is a more comprehensive precognition of our destiny, a full picture of what we can accomplish on this planet by telling our truth and following our synchronistic guidance. What results is a new, more defined sense of who we can become.

Most Birth Visions that are not part of a near-death experience seem to occur as a result of spiritual practice, through either prayer or meditation or some other activity that expands our inner opening to the divine. For example, you might be walking through a spot of rare beauty and decide to meditate. As you meditate, your ego is quieted. Afterward you can project the intention for self-clarity and focus on the inner question "What am I to do?"

At such a time, we might experience a rush of inspiration and an image, exactly like a daydream, of ourselves doing something. Often such an image is an intuitive answer to our current life question. But sometimes, as we shall see in the final chapter, the image expands and lengthens past the current situation into the longer future—revealing in more detail what one is here on earth to accomplish. All this will correspond with the general truth you know life has prepared you to tell, but will go further to reveal the best-case evolution of this truth into what can only be described as a mission.

For instance, let's say there is a young woman who already knows she wants to move from a career in marketing to a job in teaching, because her past has prepared her to help children learn to love reading. She might then expand this sense of her truth by experiencing a fuller Birth Vision—one that reveals a larger mission to create a model of her teaching technique that could be set up in classrooms everywhere. This revelation would feel like a more complete picture of where her devotion to her truth could lead if she keeps the faith.

Such a vision of her future would be accompanied by feelings of inspiration and pride. She would sense, "If I could just do that, I would be bursting with life, completely fulfilled." Experienced in this way, the Birth Vision stays in the back of our minds as a picture of possibility that helps make sense of our current question and gives depth to the everyday coincidences we experience. We gain a sense not only of having a truth to tell but also of what can happen if we tell it in the fullest possible way.

I personally experienced such a vision in 1973 while walking in the Great Smoky Mountains in Tennessee. There, I caught a glimpse of everything that would happen with *The Celestine Prophecy* twenty years later: my work leading to the writing of a book, its popularity as a description of the emerging spiritual awareness, the later efforts to save wilderness areas, everything. At first, I thought it was nothing but a fanciful pipe dream, but the memory of the vision never went away . . . and when it began to come true, I realized it had been a true Birth Vision.

HERE ON ASSIGNMENT

Now we can see the full impact that the information about the Afterlife is having on our life here on earth. The emerging spiritual awareness is based on the perception of synchronicity, and each level of this awareness gives us a better understanding of what this synchronicity is and how to engage it every day. The Afterlife gives us the highest perspective on this process: we are here on assignment, and the synchronicity we can live guides us toward the accomplishment of our mission.

Now the true importance of getting connected within, cutting through our control devices, and finding our truth to tell all becomes clear. It is the process of waking up to who we really are. The fact is, life here on earth is all about becoming more aware of our spiritual nature.

When we find the truth that is ours to tell, it will lead us to our right career and niche in society, a process that can be furthered by a Birth Vision of what our work can ultimately accomplish.

THE REALITY OF REINCARNATION

While movies, books, and research about reincarnation have become more common in today's culture, the idea remains difficult for many people. Many religions teach that we have only one life experience and then must face judgment and eternity. But this teaching doesn't really fit with modern research and experience.

There are too many examples now of children who can remember not just vague images of another lifetime but actual names and hometowns and details of a previous life that have been verified.[8] One only has to do a superficial perusal of the literature to find overwhelming evidence that we live more than one lifetime. Dr. Brian Weiss, former chairman of the Department of Psychiatry at Mount Sinai Medical Center, leads an impressive list of doctors and writers who routinely use past-life considerations in their therapies. As Dr. Weiss demonstrates in his book *Many Lives, Many Masters,* certain phobias, anxiety attacks, and other problems often originate not in early childhood, but further back—in past lives. Dr. Weiss, in fact, feels that almost anyone can begin to remember past lives through guided meditation.[9]

How is this knowledge of reincarnation helping to increase our awareness? We know that not only are we following a synchronistic journey and finding our true niche in society, but we came here intending to complete a larger mission. Well, if we are here on a mission, so is everyone else.

This raises each synchronistic encounter to a higher level. We have to assume that we came here to touch each other at just the right time as a matter of intention. But what happens if the meeting goes wrong? How many times, for instance, do we meet someone whom we have never seen or even heard of before and automatically dislike him or her at first sight? For no good reason. And what happens if we can't get past this reaction and thus fail to uplift the person or even to attempt communication?

Will we have to see all this again in our Life Review, perhaps realizing that part of our Birth Vision was to deliver our truth just in time to send this individual in a new direction? Will we have to admit that we blew it just because of an old resentment coming from a past life? These dislikes occur frequently, and it is important to work through them as quickly as possible.

WORKING THROUGH PAST-LIFE DIFFICULTIES

Once again, we can fall back on our knowledge of dealing with control dramas. In that case, the procedure is to lay out our feelings on the table and tell the person how we are feeling when we are around him—remembering to present those feelings gently and being open to the possibility that we are wrong. When dealing with sudden ill feelings toward someone else, I believe that the same process can be used. We can ask for a serious conversation and say we have an unusual reaction toward the individual and that we would like to explore where it might be originating.

Remember that we are having to overcome the momentum of the old materialistic worldview that considers such conversations awkward, embarrassing, or even silly. Another alternative is simply to arrange some later time with the person and bring the subject up then. In any case, the other person might just dismiss the matter entirely or become threatened personally by the discussion and close down.

Yet in order to maintain a higher awareness, and be-cause we know what we know, we must continue to pursue the issue. As time passes, these types of conver-sations will become easier as more individuals reach an awareness of the process. Ideally, when two people ex-plore such feelings, images of a relevant past life to-gether will surface, and from these admittedly vague ideas can come a sense of forgiveness and a new focus on the matters at hand.

According to Dr. Weiss, past-life memory is accessed in the same manner as other transcendent information: by going within. We can enter a state of meditation with the intention and prayer that we receive knowledge of the source of our feelings. We can meditate separately in this manner, but I believe that the increased energy of a group—this can be the parties involved, an experienced facilitator, or members of a regular support network—can raise the probability of success.

I suggest that you first have the group affirm that the past-life situation can be remembered. Then the group can go into silent meditation, after which each person can discuss the images and memories that surface. It is of utmost importance that everyone state what occurred in complete honesty and not confirm others' images in-appropriately.

In most cases, some agreement about the particular past-life relationships of the people involved will emerge. If one or both of the people feel as though they were harmed in some way during the past life, then, once again, apologies and forgiveness are the only ways to resolve those perceptions. Only at this point can the two people go on to understand why they have crossed paths in the present. Is it simply to resolve these old feelings? Is it to deliver a special message in this time and place? Or have they met to enter into a more long-term working relationship, a joint mission of some kind?

TOGETHER AGAIN

What about those unexplainable feelings that we have for some people that are positive? The easy sense of love that comes quickly when we meet a new person, or the sense that someone looks familiar.

We could be anywhere when suddenly a person glances our way. Immediately, we think she looks familiar, as though we met her somewhere but can't remember where. Something about her facial expressions, or maybe just the feeling of her presence, feels so right to us. If a conversation develops, we often realize that we are on the same wavelength. The words come easily and comprehension is immediate.

Once again, one of the greatest challenges of humankind is to move the interpretation of this experience away from sexuality and into the realm of the purely spiritual, especially between men and women. We must expand our awareness past the illusions of codependence to look for the synchronistic messages that pertain to our life mission.

THE EFFECT OF AFTERLIFE INFORMATION

As we have seen, the more we discover about the Afterlife dimension, the more our lives here on earth are illuminated. We know that every synchronistic moment, every meeting with another human, has implications far beyond the ordinary. All of us come to earth with a mission in mind, and each time that we are guided to just the right place, given just the right information, or uplift someone at just the right time, it feels destined, because some part of us remembers it was supposed to happen.

The overriding question is how conscious we can make these moments. Right now. Because at this point in our journey, we are on the verge of remembering everything: who we are as spiritual beings, how we came to be here, and where we are intending to go in the future.

12

VISUALIZING HUMAN DESTINY

As ever more information about the Afterlife filters into public awareness, I believe our understanding of human history and destiny will change dramatically. If each of us is born into the world on assignment, that means everyone who has ever lived has been here on assignment, and everything that has occurred has been following a higher purpose.

In fact, with this new awareness, I believe we can already sense a whole new story forming about what has happened in this dimension. We can sense this story because, in actuality, what we are doing is remembering this great sequence of events.

When the universe exploded into being, we were an aspect of what was happening. We lived in the first stars as they gravitated together, created the basic elemental energy patterns, and dispersed them throughout space.

Our intention joined the divine as the sun and other planets formed our solar system, creating the perfect environment for life on earth. We were the first amino acids as they evolved into one-celled plants and later animals. We were the plants as they liberated free oxygen into the atmosphere for the first time. We swam the oceans as multicelled organisms and then fish. It was we who yearned to push past the boundaries of the waters, celebrating as we leaped into the form of amphibians and first crawled upon the land. And we were part of the greater consciousness that moved through reptiles and mammals and finally into our own species.

From there the story proceeds as our souls patiently participated in the thousands of lifetimes that passed before humans acquired the first stirrings of self-consciousness. Slowly, we awakened and became aware that we were alive on the earth and would eventually die. Unlike the other animals, we needed to know why we were here. What was our purpose?

A SPIRITUAL HISTORY

At the moment we first asked that question, evolution entered a new arena: the slow progress of human reality toward the truth of who we are and of what we should be doing. Early mankind created rich mythology that attempted to explain our existence and how we came to be in this world. Yet from the beginning, we were short on energy, and we began to manipulate and dominate each other, beginning with the use of brute force.

We can see now that evolution had an underlying purpose for this mayhem: the dissemination of new ideas. Early humans immediately felt the drive to conquer and unify, to force others to adopt their point of view. The strongest humans dominated and won the deference and attention of the others, and in a process of slow unification, these strong individuals and their followers conquered larger and larger amounts of territory and peoples, imposing new philosophies of life—only to be conquered later themselves and beset with other values and beliefs.

From the perspective of the Afterlife, all this was simply the best we could do under the circumstances. I believe we each can intuit that we came to earth many times throughout this evolution. And every time we came, following our Birth Vision, our intention was to do everything we could to move humanity away from the barbarism of war and empire and to introduce a more civilized way to unify and discern the truth.

At first, this delivery of higher truth progressed very slowly, because in the early years the gap between what we knew in the Afterlife and what we could live on the earth was very great. Each time we were born, we struggled to overcome the conventions of the cultures we were born into, labored to remember the truth we were supposed to bring into the world. Slowly, however, the civilizing efforts of groups of inspired humans began to make a difference. In the Middle East, Jewish tribes created a rich mythology based on the idea of one God, and slowly this idea of one creator, one fatherly source shared by everyone, spread across much of the Western Hemisphere.

From the East, a similar recognition began to spread that each of us shared a common oneness with the absolute intelligence or Godhead. This idea created a leap in unification. Now rather than thinking we were supported by a local god who competed with the gods of our enemies, the awareness began to surface that all human beings were in essence part of the same creative force.

BRINGING EVOLUTION TO CONSCIOUSNESS

By the year 600 B.C., another great truth was being delivered into the world in Greece: the idea that instead of using brutality, we could relate to each other in a democratic way. Through the work of hundreds of individuals, this idea began to spread slowly into ancient Rome, and a revolutionary new idea was released into the world: instead of human affairs and evolution being pushed forward through physical domination, we could debate the merits of particular points of view. Reality could now evolve through a progression of better ideas.

In the centuries that followed, other visionaries, such as Lao-tzu, Buddha, and Jesus, began to clarify the nature of the spiritual source that we shared. Jesus declared that the kingdom of God was not outside of us somewhere, but within. And in a limited way, this idea was integrated into cultural life both in the evolving Buddhism and Taoism of the East and in the Christianity of the West.

Meanwhile, humans continued to gravitate into ever larger groups, our identification and allegiance with others growing from small bands or villages to greater regions, and then into a consciousness of specific nations with clear boundaries. Finally, beginning with the Renaissance in the West, thousands of individuals rediscovered the democratic values of antiquity and began to emphasize human dignity and basic human rights.

Many nations replaced the idea of the divine right of kings with the system of popular democracy. Amid the secular revolutions of the time, the United States was formed as a visionary but still-incomplete idea of a country where human beings would be free to pursue their deepest dreams.

As we saw in earlier chapters, science was created in the same spirit of idealism and was sent out to replace the capricious superstitions of the day. When it failed to supply a new picture of mankind's spiritual situation, an obsessive focus on outer, materialistic security prevailed.

The cultures of the East, meanwhile, continued to explore the inner world of spiritual experience and the attainment of security within. Still, the communication of ideas proceeded, pushing our social evolution even further.

By the early twentieth century, numerous individuals, unconsciously following their Birth Visions, awoke to new truths. Newton's mechanical description of the universe began to be replaced by the perspective of Einstein and the quantum physicists. Other inspired people began to awaken to the extremes of the economic obsession: breaking up cartels and monopolies in the United States, creating national parks and forests, taking a stand against imperialism, and in a small way beginning to protect the more diverse human cultures around the world.

By midcentury, millions had responded to the idea that forceful empire building must end, fighting two world wars and a long cold one, before finally implementing a consensus for protecting the rights of sovereign peoples and their national borders. Through the work of countless individuals, the idea of a United Nations organization was made a reality, marking the first time human consciousness had reached out to include all the peoples of the earth.

In recent decades, a new understanding of the

human universe has begun to emerge. The new physics describes our world in terms of energy dynamics and mysterious interconnections. Other scientists have begun to explore the full range of potential human experience, including the mystery of synchronicity, the depth of our intuition, and the powers of our intention.

We are at this moment, because of the truths millions of humans have slowly brought into the world, becoming aware of the full picture of evolution. By unconsciously following their Birth Visions, each generation throughout history has been serving to evolve human reality in a purposeful way, bringing us ever closer to the spiritual awareness that already exists in the Afterlife dimension. Step by step we are becoming aware that we are spiritual beings slowly evolving a spiritual reality on this planet.

FACING THE POLARIZATION

Just because we are creating a spiritual culture doesn't mean the job is finished. To some extent, we are still in that gray area during which one worldview has lost its ability to fully inspire us, but the next ruling paradigm has yet to reach full acceptance. In fact, in recent decades we have witnessed an extreme polarization of forces between those promoting change and those resisting it. In America, the energy of the conflict is rising as both sides sense the outcomes are critical for the future.

Facing the ever-rising sounds of what has been called by some a cultural war, public opinion has swung back and forth between the two extremes. In the 1980s, those defending the old worldview seemed to have won the day, asserting that we must go back to the realities and the values of yesteryear, when the focus was on work and family and economic progress. They felt that the problems in our culture could be traced directly to the influence of the human potential movement, whose liberal ideas resulted in the growth of government intervention, unacceptable budget deficits, fading role distinctions between men and women, leniency toward crime, and a general tendency for people to blame society for their problems.

Others countered that there would be no federal deficits if billions of dollars were not tied up in business subsidies and corporate welfare, listing a litany of abuse: federal subsidies to arms dealers to market their weapons overseas totaling $7.5 billion; $1 billion to large corporations like Continental Grain and Cargill, Inc., to provide free shipping of wheat, corn, and other commodities; $700 million for below-cost logging sales and road subsidies to timber companies cutting on national forest lands. The list goes on and on.[1]

Human potentialists maintained that the problems of the United States flowed from the extremes of the old economic focus: out-of-control pollution, a neglect of ethics in business, corporate corruption of government, a failure to educate all of our people, and a limited commitment to intervene in areas of cyclical poverty and crime.

On the most recent swing of the pendulum, which installed a Republican Congress in Washington in 1994, the public bought the conservative argument that government budgets were out of control, that public immorality and crime were expanding, and that government should be scaled back and replaced by a focus on personal integrity.

But then people began to witness inconsistencies on the part of the Republican majority, who had promised to implement reform. Before our eyes, the party began to return to its old habits—protecting big-business subsidies instead of cutting the budget fairly. And instead of making environmental protection a priority, one Republican, a former pest exterminator from Texas, proposed that parts of the Clean Water Act be repealed. This happened at a time when most of the public was hearing about our rivers and oceans growing progressively more polluted. To top it off, a salvage rider was tacked onto a popular bill that allowed large timber corporations to cut trees hundreds of years old in our national forests.

Because of these abuses, the pendulum now seems to be swinging again as the public grows ever more frustrated and cynical about politics. Meanwhile, many people caught in the no-man's-land between the old and new worldviews are growing increasingly more lost and frustrated, often lashing out in mindless desperation. Violence in our streets and homes explodes daily. Terrorists and antigovernment extremists carry out crazed wars in their minds.

In some ways, this is the inevitable darkness before the dawn. Yet I believe that from the perspective of the new awareness, our course is clearly marked.

PERCEIVING THE WORLD VISION

Just as we can go within and remember our Birth Vision, we can go back to that place of wisdom and remember the larger intention that has motivated history. Whether through prayer or meditation, or walks through the energy of an unspoiled, sacred site, we can remember the shared World Vision, a vision of the future human world we are moving to create.

I believe that we have always known this moment would come: the time when we could fully bring into consciousness our evolutionary goal and then all work together in full awareness to get there. I believe that the first event we see in our vision is a great wave building at this moment in history, pushed forward by individuals who can see a positive future.

What's more, we can see the first course of action—to resolve the polarization of opinion that blocks our continued evolution—and precisely how to accomplish this task. If we look at the situation from the perspective of our new spiritual awareness, we can see that while some people are resisting the building of a spiritual culture on earth because of fear, most are resisting because of a deep-seated intuition that many important values held in the old worldview are in danger of being lost in the transition.

They seem to be worrying that in our efforts to liberate human potential, too much power is moving to centralized governments around the world, and we are losing the important values of personal initiative and self-reliance and responsibility. And we must assume that they are voicing the truth of their Birth Visions as they express this concern. We can see, then, that to resolve the polarization, we must begin to integrate the best ideas of both sides.

We can also see, I believe, that this can occur as the wave of new awareness begins to affect the political forces aligned on one side or the other. Think tanks, news organizations, and politicians themselves will find higher perspective on these issues. For instance, we might look at the national budget. This issue is not just about deficits, it is about corrupt appropriations and tax loopholes that benefit special interests at the expense of the public good.

These problems can be resolved very quickly if all politicians rise to the occasion and divorce themselves from the special interests that seek unfair privilege. I believe that it would only take a reputable group of states-men and stateswomen, perhaps retired, to hold weekly press conferences—naming names, exposing special-interest legislation—to turn public sentiment around. Republicans must end the welfare given to business and corporate constituencies. Democrats must comb through the maze of social welfare systems, including entitlements to the wealthy elderly, and keep only those that are genuinely fair.

But what about the rest of human society? Again, synchronicity has been moving millions of individuals inspired by the new awareness into precisely the right position to accomplish their missions, and now we can see the larger vision of what we want to happen. The heroes are all in place, and the heroes are us. We'll suddenly look out on our profession, our office, our job, and we'll say, this place is not functioning at its highest level of purpose.

Or we'll look out at a social problem and think, this is not right, someone ought to do something. In that moment, we'll realize what we wanted to happen, what our World Vision makes clear. In all such cases, the person to do something, to intervene, is you.

And because we understand the dynamics of energy competition, these interventions can take place with less hostility and more inspired cooperation. Sometimes, quite unexpectedly, we'll find others who are there just to help us. And we'll even remember that we planned together, before birth, to come to this location to reform a particular situation or institution.

Thus we can all remember in a higher way that we intended, at this time in history, for there to be a great wave of inspired action that would sweep across the planet, addressing all of the world's current problems.

OVERCOMING POVERTY AND WORLD HUNGER

Our wave of intervention toward poverty and hunger will move forward by integrating two important truths. Stalwarts of the old paradigm have long maintained that these problems cannot be solved by uninspired, secularly oriented bureaucrats using an abstract formula. All that occurs during this kind of intervention, in their view, is a growing dependence by those in poverty on government handouts. Yet too often those in the old paradigm have used this argument as an excuse to do nothing.

Now, however, I believe we can see that the old paradigm proponents have been correct in emphasizing personal responsibility, but human potentialists have also been correct in intuiting that a way exists to help. I believe our higher vision now reveals to us what we can do.

The key to resolving cycles of poverty in families is to intervene in a personal way. Government programs will never work as anything other than a safety net. Hundreds of thousands of us will find ourselves in the position to intervene with a family stuck in dire circumstances or poverty. Volunteer organizations such as Big Brothers, Big Sisters, as well as groups dedicated to ending world hunger, will increase in size, but the greatest volunteerism will come spontaneously from the person down the street, who will befriend a child or inspire a family. This is a truth now emerging into consciousness, and the recent emphasis on volunteerism led by General Colin Powell and two former presidents is just the beginning.[2]

Poverty, wherever it is occurring in the world, is a situation fueled by fear, undereducation, and a failure to take advantage of opportunities that come one's way. The solution is for a wave of individuals who are living synchronistically to intervene personally with those stuck in self-defeating patterns. Just through interacting, we can model a new way of pursuing life that the family members in poverty can apply to their own situations.

Remember, in this connected universe of ours, we have the potential to share minds, and our new awareness is transferred quite literally by contagion. Discovering synchronicity, connecting with an inner divine energy, clearing repeated patterns, and breaking free to find one's own miraculous journey into the future works for every human being, regardless of the situation.

PREVENTING CRIME

The problem of crime is more difficult, but it will respond in exactly the same way if we integrate the best of another polarized set of beliefs. In the United States forty years ago, street crime was approached with zero tolerance. Street people were rounded up and jailed for vagrancy, and police had virtually absolute power. It was the work of those believing in human rights that reformed this system so that it could operate more in accordance with the Constitution. Yet those defending the old paradigm often see the emphasis in the last thirty years on the rights of the accused, the social genesis of deviancy, and the need for rehabilitation as having undermined law enforcement and led to a subsequent explosion in levels of crime.

What we can see now, I believe, is that in part this belief is correct. An emphasis on social intervention by bureaucracies has indeed led to a dropping of standards, especially when overcrowded prisons and sympathetic judges led to an increase in early releases or outright leniency. The message on the street was that crime—white-collar or otherwise—was not taken seriously and was even excused. What we are finding now—as recent no-tolerance approaches in many of our major cities are proving—is that effective crime intervention must be backed up by a "tough love" standard that violence and crime will not be tolerated.

But tough standards do not work by themselves. The

values of the human potentialists must be applied as well. Most of the recent programs that have been successful have coupled a firmer stance with more community policemen who work in one local area, getting to know the families and their problems, and who can thereby prevent much crime.[3]

The current approaches by law enforcement are only the beginning. I believe our vision is to again address the problem with a wave of committed individuals following their own synchronicity. The beat cop can't do it all. And in most cases of crime, either planned or as the result of rage, someone knows it is about to happen, and again, that someone is the person in the best position to act. Certainly, care must be taken to remain personally safe and to notify professionals when appropriate, but often words of encouragement or a helping suggestion early in the process can prevent an extreme situation later. Again, all this will occur in the flow of synchronicity, and an even larger number of individuals will answer the call.

PROTECTING THE ENVIRONMENT

In a similar fashion, we will resolve the world's environmental problems. Waves of inspired individuals will suddenly realize that they are in exactly the right position to take action.

Water and air pollution continues to worsen, as tons of toxic chemicals are dumped into the environment each year. In addition, new chemicals are constantly invented by industry and introduced into the biosphere with little or no regulation, much of it used as pesticides and herbicides on the world's food supply.[4]

The problem is so bad that the American Medical Association has warned that pregnant mothers and infants should not eat vegetables that are mass-produced in the United States.[5] Dr. Andrew Weil, quickly becoming a national medical spokesman, advises against eating shellfish or deep-water ocean fish because their bodies now contain so many toxic chemicals, and he further recommends buying only organically produced foods. He warns that many untested chemicals, when combined with each other, become more toxic than ever imagined.[6] This is the only prudent action in a world where cancer rates are inexplicably increasing.

The pollution of our environment, especially illegal dumping and the indiscriminate use of untested chemicals, is always perpetrated by just a few people in authority. As the wave of the new spiritual awareness moves into society, these actions will be increasingly observed and some inspired individual will blow the whistle. Illegal dumping, for example, always happens in some specific place at the edge of oceans or in our rivers and sewers. As more of us are guided by synchronicity, people will be inspired to watch over every inch of shoreline and every river. If wastes are dumped in the dead of night, someone will be there—following intuition and ready to sound the alarm. In this way, legions of inspired citizens, armed with video recorders, will focus public attention on this pollution.

SAVING THE FORESTS

One of the most tragic crimes against our planet is deforestation. From an environmental point of view alone, considering the role of forests in producing the world's oxygen, this situation is alarming. But other dangers and monumental costs flow from this destruction. Human beings continue to migrate to cities and concrete suburbs devoid of the magical energy of the wilderness. Especially in the United States, wilderness areas are continually being destroyed by development and corruption.

Most American citizens don't realize that timber and mining companies are being subsidized by the American taxpayer to pillage the forests on our public lands. Not only does the Forest Service use public funds to build roads into some of the last remaining wilderness areas, creating a subsidy for large multinational corporations, but then it sells timber and minerals at below-market rates. Timber companies are notorious for running sentimental ads claiming to be managing our forests and planting more trees than they cut. But in fact they are clear-cutting old cathedral forests that have a rich diversity of plants, animals, and energy, and replacing them with sterile rows of pine trees, creating a farm, not a forest. Another problem is outright timber theft by companies who cut more timber than is sold and even fail to pay for their original bids.[7] Retiring Forest Service administrators are often hired by the very companies they used to regulate, creating a chummy, look-the-other-way attitude on the part of the Forest Service.

Fortunately, we can see the layers of governmental corruption that perpetuate this corporate welfare. And we can see the solution, a wave of concerned citizens speaking out to end this corruption and supporting legislation and reform organizations. When enough people know this corruption is occurring, it will be stopped very quickly.

WARFARE AND TERRORISM

What about the world problem of sectional warfare and terrorism? As we've seen in Bosnia and other hot spots, long-standing conflicts are motivated by religious and ethnic hatred—and they are always kept alive by individuals and small groups who are personally alienated and fearful. In these cases, some use their obsession with the conflict to ward off the anxiety of death and give their lives meaning. Other terrorist activities around the world are perpetrated for exactly the same reason: They are part of a group obsession with a cause.

I believe we can see in our World Vision that eventually our new spiritual awareness will reach these individuals as well. Inspired individuals will meet and get to know those on the fringes of such terrorist and violent separatist groups, and slowly the higher level of energy will influence friends who personally know those at the core of these conflicts. These friends will find that their higher mission is to help the terrorists wake up and stop the senseless violence.

TRANSFORMING CULTURE

Our World Vision doesn't stop with an intervention into our social problems. The everyday operation of every aspect of human life will be impacted by the growing wave of individuals living the new consciousness. The economy will begin to transform as we introduce tithing as a supplement to normal commerce. Business activity will continue to progress as those who have small companies begin to move their decision making toward a more ideal level of functioning.

Capitalism has proved to be the most functional human economic system. Why? Because it is oriented toward providing the needs of human beings, and because it allows a constant inflow of new information and technology to be arranged in ever more productive ways, shifting and changing in response to our consciousness. In short, it evolves.

Corruptions of capitalism occur when people are vulnerable to excessive advertising that seeks to create needs based on insecurity, or when the operation of the marketplace fails to adequately protect consumers or the environment. Ideally, these problems are solved if people who are in business focus on truly providing for human needs, rather than purely on maximizing profits. I believe that we can see ourselves moving toward this ideal. Because of the growing spiritual awareness of people in business, and because they find themselves perfectly placed to make a difference, more and more of us are beginning to see ourselves as serving a higher vision of the future.

In part, this shift is occurring at a time when business ethics seem to be at an all-time low, and when companies are locked into thinking only about short-term profits. But our growing awareness of this venality is shocking us into reform. Public opinion will force the pendulum of business in the other direction. Companies that actually factor in environmental costs and meet the needs of the consumer will win favor. And slowly, because of our expanding awareness of where human evolution is taking us, companies will begin to think long-term again.

Planned obsolescence (the practice of designing products to break down after a period of time) will be replaced by an ethic of making products that will last a lifetime, at the lowest possible cost—because, once again, our evolution is taking us toward an economy where our material needs will ultimately be fully automated and freely available, moving our focus to the exchange of spiritual information.

Of course, as we noted, to make all this possible we must discover a low-cost, renewable source of energy, and new materials that are inexpensive and durable. According to numerous scientists, we seem to be moving closer to perfecting cold fusion. Although paradigm battles still rage around this discovery (cold fusion seems to work in a way that defies our older physical theories), I believe that our intuition tells us that ultimately we will find an unlimited, renewable source.

Certainly, various corporations, deeply invested in oil and gas production, will fight against its development. But the wave of inspired people who will work to implement the truth will be unstoppable. Scientists will find that this is exactly the area that gives their lives the most meaning and purpose, and aware journalists will disseminate information to the public before it can be suppressed.

OCCUPATIONS AND PROFESSIONS

Our World Vision shows us, I believe, that every occupation and profession will also transform. Already in many areas of human society, reform associations are being created to monitor ethical standards. Within the medical profession, for instance, associations of practitioners are working to promote preventive techniques designed to head off disease before it starts, rather than merely to react with drugs and sometimes unnecessary surgery.[8]

Similar reforms are under way in the legal profession. Lawyers are perfectly placed to help resolve conflicts between people, to provide win-win solutions to problems. Unfortunately, the public has experienced just the opposite action from most lawyers, finding that they often inflame the situation, take cases to court unnecessarily, and extend the difficulty between people for as long as possible—merely to earn higher fees. Few professions have been held in lower regard. Yet there are associations of lawyers dedicated to reforming these corrupt practices and to moving the legal profession toward a more ideal level of functioning.[9]

In this way, all the professions and occupations will begin to shift. Accountants will become ever more effective teachers of money management. Both family and corporate farmers will grow food organically, in ways that preserve the soil, build up vitamins and minerals in their crops, and leave them unpolluted with the residue of chemical pesticides. Restaurant owners will move toward serving only this high-energy, clean food, preserving its nutritional value. Journalists will move away from sensationalism and toward a spiritually based, substantive vision. And builders and developers will begin to preserve the last remaining natural areas and to replant other areas. We will all want to live as close to a high-energy wilderness as possible and to have ever more green parks and walking areas around our commercial developments. In the end, every institution will evolve toward its greatest role of service, facilitating the new spiritual awareness everywhere.

MERGING THE DIMENSIONS

I believe that our World Vision shows us that human beings will continue to increase their personal energy levels. During the evolution of our business practices and goals, and the transformation of our professional and occupational roles, we will be guided on our way by synchronistic moments, filling us with ever higher levels of inspiration and energy.

As greater numbers of people increase their energy, these will be the energy levels expected in the culture, and life spans will begin to lengthen dramatically. As we work to stabilize world population levels, inspired couples will forgo having children of their own to adopt parentless children from around the globe.

Over time, we will have gradually automated our survival needs, regrown the depleted forests, and returned much of the land back to wilderness. We will live in homes that are infinitely durable and inexhaustibly powered. At this point, our mission will be to grow spiritually and focus on the increase in energy itself. Here the synchronistic moments will be even more inspiring as we meet others along some wooded path or beneath a five-hundred-year-old oak that lives beside the stream. Again, these meetings will occur at exactly the right times for our lives to evolve to a higher level of energy.

At the same time, contact with angels and departed loved ones who are already in the Afterlife will increase, completing a trend that is already under way.[10] Death will be known as a transition to a dimension that is increasingly familiar and nonthreatening. And eventually, as the quantum energy patterns of our bodies begin to increase to ever higher levels, we will find ourselves in purely spiritual form. We will still be standing right where we are, by the stream again or under the old oak, but we will be able to see our bodies for what they have always been—pure light.

Here, finally, illuminated by our World Vision, I believe we can see the full purpose of life's historical journey on earth. As aspects of the divine consciousness, we came here to slowly manifest the spiritual consciousness of the Afterlife in this dimension. From the big bang to the complex organic atoms and molecules, from one-celled plants and animals to human beings, we moved forward. Through the work of thousands of generations, and millions of individuals courageous enough to deliver their inspired truths, we have slowly worked to live an awareness that we knew, but had to remember while in human form.

Our overriding purpose has been to raise our energy level to the point where we can walk into the Afterlife dimension, essentially merging the two dimensions into one. Interestingly, we will see that the angels and other souls have always been right here, just out of sight, working tirelessly to help us achieve the level of awareness that dissolves the veil.

HOLDING THE VISION

As we look around in the last days of the twentieth century, we know that we have not yet reached our destiny. In fact, for many, this book will seem overly idealistic if not fanciful. The assumptions and fears of the old secular worldview pull at us still, cloaking us with the illusion that nothing so magical could possibly be happening, and luring us into the false security of skepticism and denial.

Our challenge, then, is to put our awareness into action, to keep the faith. As we have seen, all that has been gained in history has been accomplished by heroic individuals pushing forward against often overwhelming odds. Yet now, as never before, we find ourselves at a crossroads. In the years ahead, science will complete its redefining of the outer universe and our relationship with it, and what will be confirmed is the amazing extent of our creative abilities.

We are, in our essence, conscious fields of intention, and what we think we know, what we believe, is broadcast outward into the midst of everyone else, and into the cosmos which, to a great extent, gives us the future we imagine. As our awareness of this ability grows, our power will be increased, and our ethical decisions will be empowered.

In the future earth, we will be able to manifest almost anything our egos might dream up—and so, as never before, we must be careful what we wish for. We must watch our thoughts because negative images, like stray bullets, go out and do harm. Thankfully, all the great mystics of history, as well as our most sacred scriptures, have thoroughly warned us: We must always go within to our highest wisdom to chart our path in life. Each of us must find our own confirmation of a World Vision that follows not from fear or scarcity, but from some greater part of our memory.

Once we find that vision, the exciting work begins. Not only does this vision center us in courage as we pursue our individual missions, it takes us to the highest point of our new spiritual awareness, the point at which it can serve as the basis for everything we do. All we have to do to remain centered in this awareness, to live it every day, is to hold this inner vision.

Before we go out of the house, we must find that space, that spiritual posture, in which we live what we know. The power of faith is real. Every thought is a prayer, and if the vision of the new spiritual awareness resides in the back of our minds every day, every minute, as we interact in the world, the magic of synchronicity will accelerate for everyone, and the destiny we intuit in our hearts will become a reality.

NOTES

PREFACE

1. G. Celente, *Trends 2000* (New York: Warner, 1997).

2. N. Herbert, *Quantum Reality: Beyond the New Physics* (New York: Anchor/Doubleday, 1985).

3. F. Capra, *Turning Point* (New York: Bantam, 1987).

4. E. Becker, *The Denial of Death* (New York: Free Press, 1973).

5. W. James, *The Varieties of Religious Experience* (New York: Random House, 1994); C. Jung, *Modern Man in Search of a Soul* (New York: Harcourt Brace, 1955); H. D. Thoreau, *On Walden Pond* (New York: Borders Press, 1994); R. W. Emerson, *Complete Works* (Irvine, Calif.: Reprint Services, 1992); A. Huxley, *Huxley and God* (San Francisco: HarperSanFrancisco, 1992); G. Leonard, *The Transformation* (Los Angeles: J. P. Tarcher, 1987); M. Murphy, *The Future of the Body* (Los Angeles: J. P. Tarcher, 1992); F. Capra, *The Tao of Physics* (Boulder, Colo.: Bantam, 1976); M. Ferguson, *The Aquarian Conspiracy* (New York: J. P. Tarcher/Put-

nam, 1980); L. Dossey, *Recovering the Soul* (New York: Bantam, 1989).

CHAPTER 1

1. J. C. Pearce, *Crack in the Cosmic Egg* (New York: Pocket, 1971).
2. N. O. Brown, *Life against Death* (Hanover, N.H.: Wesleyan Univ. Press, 1985); A. Maslow, *Farther Reaches of Human Nature* (New York: Viking/Penguin, 1993); *Religions, Values and Peak Experiences* (New York: Viking/Penguin, 1994).
3. K. Horney, *Neurosis and Human Growth* (New York: W. W. Norton, 1993).

CHAPTER 2

1. I. Progoff, *Jung: Synchronicity and Human Destiny* (New York: Julian Press, 1993).
2. C. Jung, *Synchronicity* (New York: Bollingen/Princeton Univ. Press, 1960).
3. F. D. Peat, *Synchronicity: The Bridge between Matter and Mind* (New York: Bantam, 1987).
4. M. A. Carskadon, editor, *Encyclopedia of Sleep and Dreaming* (New York: Macmillan, 1993).
5. A. Robbins, . . . *with Deepak Chopra,* taped interview, Guthy-Renker, 1993.
6. E. Becker, *Escape from Evil* (New York: Free Press, 1985).

CHAPTER 3

1. E. Becker, *The Structure of Evil* (New York: George Braziller, 1968).
2. T. Cahill, *How the Irish Saved Civilization* (New York: Anchor/Doubleday, 1995).

3. A. Koestler, *The Sleepwalkers* (New York: Grosset & Dunlap, 1963).

4. F. Capra, *Turning Point* (New York: Bantam, 1987).

5. E. Becker, *The Denial of Death* (New York: Free Press, 1973).

CHAPTER 4

1. T. S. Kuhn, *The Structure of Scientific Revolutions* (Chicago: Univ. of Chicago Press, 1970).

2. F. Capra, *The Tao of Physics* (Boulder, Colo.: Bantam, 1976).

3. M. Kaku and J. Trainen, *Beyond Einstein* (New York: Bantam, 1987).

4. N. Herbert, *Quantum Reality: Beyond the New Physics* (New York: Anchor/Doubleday, 1985).

5. M. Kaku, *Hyperspace* (New York: Oxford Univ. Press, 1994).

6. Herbert, *Quantum Reality*.

7. Ibid.

8. Kaku, *Hyperspace*.

9. R. Leakey, *The Origin of Humankind* (New York: Basic Books/HarperCollins, 1994).

10. M. Murphy, *The Future of the Body* (Los Angeles: J. P. Tarcher, 1992).

11. F. Goble, *The Third Force* (Pasadena, Calif.: Thomas Jefferson Center, 1970).

12. I. Progoff, *Jung: Synchronicity and Human Destiny* (New York: Julian Press, 1993).

13. R. D. Laing, *The Divided Self* (New York: Pantheon, 1969).

14. E. Berne, *Games People Play* (New York: Ballantine, 1985); T. Harris, *I'm OK/You're OK* (New York: HarperCollins, 1969).

15. P. Teilhard de Chardin, *The Phenomenon of Man* (San Bernardino, Calif.: Borgo Press, 1994); Sri Aurobindo, *Major Works of Sri Aurobindo* (Lodi, Calif.: Auromere, 1990).

16. *Biofeedback: A Source Guide* (New York: Gordon Press, 1991).

17. L. Dossey, *Healing Words* (New York: HarperCollins, 1993).

18. L. Dossey, *Recovering the Soul* (New York: Bantam, 1989).

19. Dossey, *Healing Words.*

20. Dossey, *Recovering the Soul.*

21. Ibid.

22. L. Dossey, *Be Careful What You Pray For, You Just Might Get It* (San Francisco: HarperSanFrancisco, 1997).

CHAPTER 5

1. R. D. Laing, *Self and Others* (New York: Pantheon, 1970).

2. E. Berne, *Games People Play* (New York: Ballantine, 1985).

3. J. Q. Wilson and R. J. Herrnstein, *Crime and Human Nature: The Definitive Study of the Causes of Crime* (New York: Touchstone/Simon & Schuster, 1985).

4. J. Hillman, *We Had a Hundred Years of Psychotherapy—and the World's Getting Worse* (San Francisco: HarperSanFrancisco, 1992).

CHAPTER 6

1. C. Jung, *Psychology and Religion* (New Haven, Conn.: Yale Univ. Press, 1938); A. W. Watts, *Psychotherapy East and West* (New York: Random House, 1975); D. T. Suzuki, *Introduction to Zen* (New York: Grove/Atlantic, 1987).

2. P. Yogananda, *Autobiography of a Yogi* (Los Angeles: Self Realization Fellowship, 1974); J. Krishnamurti, *Think on These*

Things (New York: Random House, 1975); R. Dass, *Be Here Now* (San Cristobal, N.M.: Lama Foundation, 1971).

3. G. K. Chesterton, *St. Francis of Assisi* (New York: Doubleday, 1987); M. Eckhart, *Treatises and Sermons of Meister Eckhart* (New York: Hippocrene, 1983); E. Swedenborg, *Scientific and Philosophical Treatises* (West Chester, Pa.: Swedenborg Foundation, 1991); E. Bucke, *Cosmic Consciousness* (Secaucus, N.J.: Carol Publishing Group, 1969).

4. S. P. Springer and G. Deutsch, *Left Brain, Right Brain* (New York: W. H. Freeman, 1981).

5. M. Murphy, *Golf in the Kingdom* (New York: Penguin Books, 1972).

6. A. W. Watts, *Way of Zen* (New York: Mentor/New American Library, 1957); *Wisdom of Insecurity* (New York: Random House, 1968).

CHAPTER 7

1. J. Hillman, *The Soul's Code* (New York: Random House, 1996).

2. D. Gaines, *Teenage Wasteland: America's Dead End Kids* (New York: HarperCollins, 1992).

3. M. Williamson, *A Return to Love* (New York: HarperCollins, 1992).

4. B. Weiss, *Many Lives, Many Masters* (New York: Simon & Schuster, 1988).

5. W. W. Dyer, *What Do You Really Want for Your Children?* (New York: William Morrow, 1985).

CHAPTER 8

1. C. Sagan, *A Demon Haunted World* (New York: Random House, 1995).

2. M. Murphy, *The Future of the Body*, Appendix A (Los Angeles: J. P. Tarcher, 1992).

3. K. Horney, *The Neurotic Personality of Our Time* (New York: W. W. Norton, 1993).

4. P. Koch-Sheras, *Dream Sourcebook: An Eye Opening Guide to Dream History, Theory and Interpretation* (Los Angeles: Lowell House, 1995).

5. Murphy, *The Future of the Body.*

6. S. MacLaine, *Out on a Limb* (New York: Bantam, 1993).

7. Murphy, *The Future of the Body.*

8. V. Frankl, *Man's Search for Meaning* (New York: Buccaneer, 1993).

CHAPTER 9

1. M. McLuhan, *The Medium Is the Message* (New York: Simon & Schuster, 1989).

2. M. Buber, *I and Thou* (New York: Simon & Schuster, 1984).

3. M. Shaw, *Group Dynamics* (New York: McGraw-Hill, 1980.)

4. B. Stokes, *Helping Ourselves: Local Solutions to Global Problems* (New York: Norton, 1981).

5. J. Sanford, *Invisible Partner* (Mahwah, N.J.: Paulist Press, 1980).

6. M. Beattie, *Codependent No More* (New York: Harper-Hazelden, 1987).

7. H. Hendrix, *Getting the Love You Want* (New York: HarperCollins, 1990); *Keeping the Love You Find* (New York: Pocket, 1993).

8. H. Schucman and W. Thetford, *A Course in Miracles* (Glen Ellen, Calif.: Foundation for Inner Peace, 1976).

CHAPTER 10

1. C. Fillmore, *Prosperity* (Lee's Summit, Mo.: Unity, 1995); *Atom Smashing Power of the Mind* (Lee's Summit, Mo.: Unity, 1995); N. Hill, *Master Key to Riches* (New York: Fawcett, 1986);

You Can Work Your Own Miracles (New York: Fawcett, 1996); N. V. Peale, *In God We Trust* (Nashville, Tenn.: Thomas Nelson, 1995); *God's Way to the Good Life* (New Canaan, Conn.: Keats, 1974).

2. J. Rifkin, *The End of Work* (New York: J. P. Tarcher/Putnam, 1995).

3. *Wall Street Journal,* "Work & Family," special supplement, March 31, 1997.

4. E. F. Mallove, "Is New Physics Needed," *Infinite Energy Magazine,* November/December 1996.

5. W. Greider, *One World, Ready or Not* (New York: Simon & Schuster, 1997).

6. R. Gerber, *Vibrational Medicine* (Santa Fe, N.M.: Bear & Co., 1988).

7. M. Murphy, *The Future of the Body* (Los Angeles: J. P. Tarcher, 1992).

CHAPTER 11

1. Gallup Poll, 1991 (Roper Center, University of Connecticut).

2. K. Ring, *Heading toward Omega* (New York: Quill/William Morrow, 1984); M. Morse, *Transformed by the Light* (New York: Ballantine/Random House, 1992).

3. Morse, *Transformed by the Light.*

4. E. Becker, *Escape from Evil* (New York: Free Press, 1985).

5. R. A. Monroe, *Journeys out of the Body* (New York: Anchor/Doubleday, 1977).

6. R. Montgomery, *A World Beyond* (New York: Fawcett Crest/Ballantine, 1985).

7. Ring, *Heading toward Omega.*

8. I. Stevenson, *Children Who Remember Previous Lives* (Charlottesville, Va.: University Press, 1987).

9. B. Weiss, *Many Lives, Many Masters* (New York: Simon & Schuster, 1988).

CHAPTER 12

1. M. Ivins, "Long and Short of Corporate Welfare," *Minneapolis Star Tribune,* December 1, 1994.

2. D. Boyett, "Summit May Point toward Better Future," *Orlando Sentinel,* April 27, 1997.

3. M. F. Pols, "City Officials Encourage Efforts for Community Based Policing," *Los Angeles Times,* January 17, 1995.

4. P. Hawken, *The Ecology of Commerce* (New York: HarperBusiness, 1993).

5. S. Gilbert, "America Tackles the Pesticide Crisis," *New York Times,* October 8, 1989.

6. A. Weil, *Optimum Health* (New York: Knopf, 1997).

7. T. P. Healy, "Dividends Reaped from Investing in Environment," *Indianapolis Star,* October 6, 1996.

8. American Holistic Medical Association, Raleigh, N.C.; American Association of Naturopathic Physicans, Seattle; Canadian Naturopathic Association, Etobicoke, Ontario; Physicians' Association for Anthroposophical Medicine, Portland, Ore.; Weleda, Inc., Congers, N.Y.; World Research Foundation, Sherman Oaks, Calif.

9. Anthroposophical Society in America, Chicago; Envision Associates, Chestnut Ridge, N.Y.; ADR Options, Philadelphia; Coast to Coast Mediation Center, Encinitas, Calif.

10. B. and J. Guggenheim, *Hello from Heaven* (New York: Bantam, 1995).